Conflict and Development

Organisational Adaptation in Conflict Situations

Mark Adams
and
Mark Bradbury

An Oxfam Working Paper

Oxfam (UK and Ireland)

Practical Action Publishing Ltd
25 Albert Street, Rugby, Warwickshire, CV21 2SD, UK
www.practicalactionpublishing.com

First published by Oxfam UK and Ireland in 1995 with ACORD, Responding to Conflict,
and the University of Birmingham

Digitized 2010 and reprinted by Practical Action Publishing
Reprinted 1998, 1999, 2001, 2018

A catalogue record for this book is available from the British Library & Library of Congress

ISBN 978-0-85598-320-8 Paperback
ISBN 978-0-85598-682-7 Digital book

Citation: Adams, M. (1995) Conflict and Development: Organisational adaptation in conflict situations, UK: Oxfam GB
https://doi.org/10.3362/9780855986827

Since 1974, Practical Action Publishing has published and disseminated books and information in support of
international development work throughout the world. All print editions are produced and distributed via ethical and
sustainable print on demand global facilities.

Practical Action Publishing is a trading name of Practical Action Publishing Ltd (Company Reg. No. 01159018 | VAT
880 9924 76). All profits are covenanted back to its parent group, Practical Action (Charity Reg. No. 247257).

The views and opinions in this publication are those of the author and do not represent those of
Practical Action Publishing Ltd or its parent charity Practical Action. Reasonable efforts have been made to publish
reliable data and information, but the author and publisher cannot assume responsibility for the validity of all materials
or for the consequences of their use.

The manufacturer's authorised representative in the EU for product safety is Lightning Source France, 1 Av. Johannes
Gutenberg, 78310 Maurepas, France. compliance@lightningsource.fr

CONTENTS

PREAMBLE

The growing incidence of armed conflicts in Africa and Eastern Europe, and their devastating impact, has placed conflict at the forefront of policy debates on aid and development. In the last years of the millennium the protection of human rights and livelihoods, the promotion of development in situations of conflict, and the building of 'sustainable peace' are, perhaps, the major challenges facing the global community.

This paper was prepared as a background document for the *Development in Conflict* workshop, held in Birmingham, UK, 1–3 November, 1994. The workshop was convened by ACORD, Birmingham University's School of Public Policy, and Responding to Conflict. Funds for the preparation of the paper were supplied by the Centre for Urban and Regional Studies, and the Development Administration Group, Birmingham University.

The theme of the workshop was *Organisational Adaptation in Conflict Situations*. The escalation of armed conflicts since the 1980s, the collapse of governments and the weakening of sovereignty, have created new, often life-threatening, operating environments for non-governmental organisations (NGOs),and bilateral and multilateral agencies working for the alleviation of poverty and the relief of suffering. Many of the agencies working in this new environment are adapting policies, practices, and organisational structures to meet the new challenges. The aim of the workshop was to bring together development practitioners, policy analysts and makers to share experiences and analysis of the current adaptations that organisations and institutions are making when working in situations of armed conflict.

This paper draws together current thinking on the causes and impacts of current armed conflicts. Many of the ideas presented in this paper are unlikely to be new to readers. It was hoped that the workshop would identify the gaps and develop some new lines of analysis.

The paper is illustrated with extracts from case studies on the work of the ACORD in Africa and much of the paper focuses on current NGO experience in Africa.[1] It was hoped that workshop participants with knowledge of other parts of the globe would add their insights and broaden the discourse. In addition, it was intended that the workshop would also move beyond the experience of NGOs to incorporate the strategies of the United Nations, donors, governmental agencies, and human rights organisations working in situations of conflict.

As the debate on aid and conflict cannot be held in isolation from discussion of mainstream development policy, there is a need to broaden the debate on development in conflict beyond the large-scale wars and 'complex emergencies' to the daily conflicts, disputes, and insecurities that people face in 'peaceful' situations.

The workshop suggested a series of questions that aid organisations working in situations of armed conflict need to address. These are found in later sections of the paper. Discussions during the workshop highlighted the uncertainty and doubt that exist within agencies over recent responses to the growing incidence of armed conflict. As a result, the conclusions were tentative, and it was felt that we are still some way from a full understanding of this new environment.

A conference report is to be published shortly, but it was felt that the theme paper would serve as a timely and useful resource for those grappling with the problems of working in situations of armed conflict. Oxfam has published the paper in its Discussion Paper series, as offering a valuable contribution to the debate on these difficult and urgent issues.

Acknowledgements

This paper was commissioned by ACORD, Birmingham University's School of Public Policy, and Responding to Conflict. The authors are grateful to the following people for their comments on various drafts of the paper: Judy El Bushra, Simon Fisher, Judith Gardner, Chris Roche, Andrew Shepherd, Bridget Walker, and Tina Wallace.

We are greateful to Nationale Comissie Voorlichting en Bewustwording Ontwikkelingssamenwerking for permission to reproduce the map overleaf.

About the authors

Mark Adams is currently Assistant Research and Policy Officer with ACORD, with specific responsibility for conflict issues. Previously he has travelled and worked in Central America and Africa.

Mark Bradbury has worked extensively in Africa with non-governmental development and relief programmes. He has trained in conflict analysis and has published on Somalia and Somaliland.

Wars and Armed Conflicts in 1993

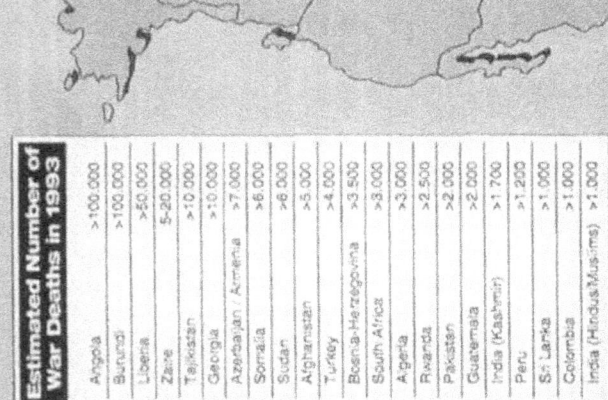

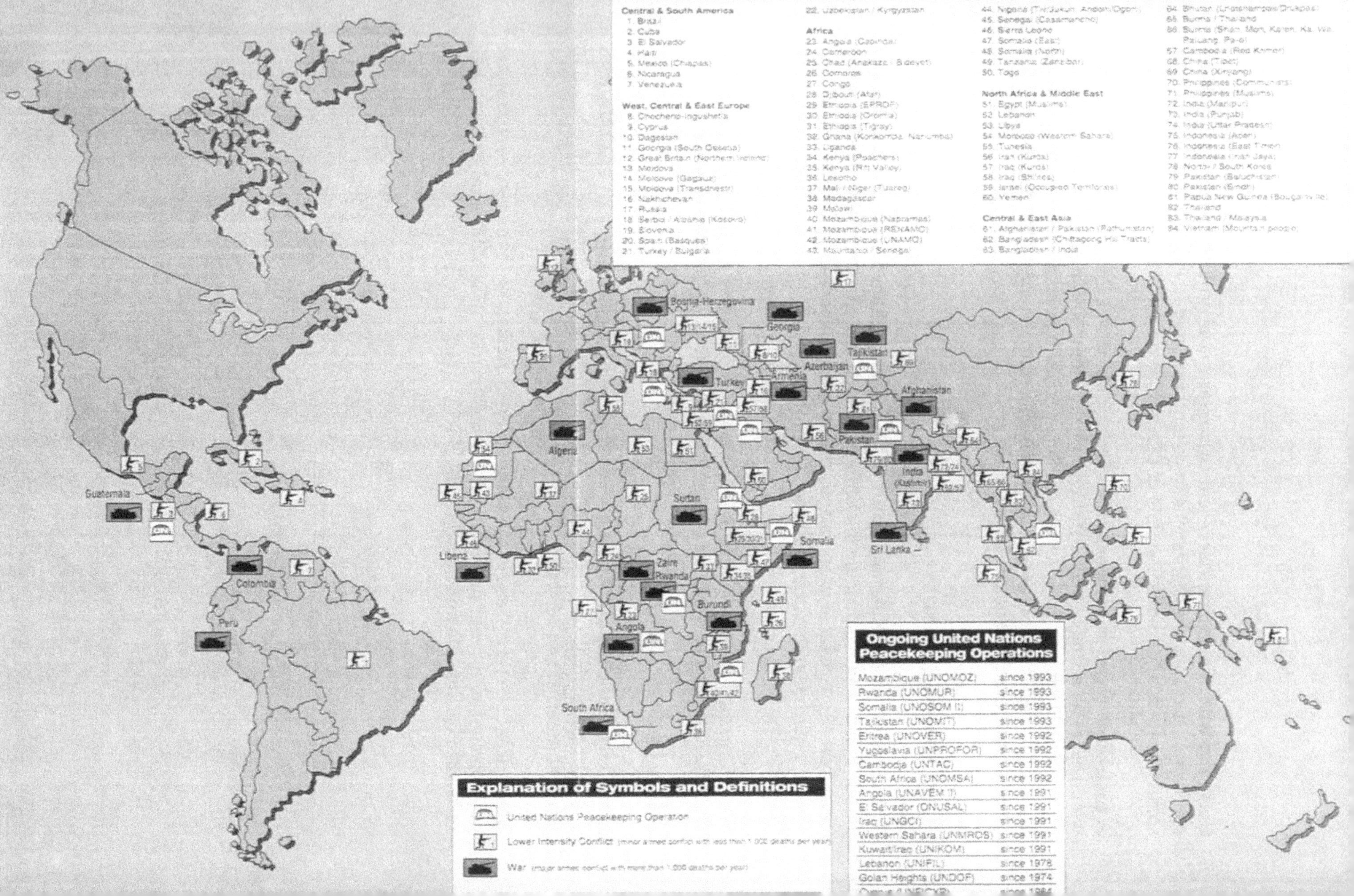

Lower Intensity Conflicts

Central & South America
1. Brazil
2. Cuba
3. El Salvador
4. Haiti
5. Mexico (Chiapas)
6. Nicaragua
7. Venezuela

West, Central & East Europe
8. Chechenia-Ingushetia
9. Cyprus
10. Dagestan
11. Georgia (South Ossetia)
12. Great Britain (Northern Ireland)
13. Moldova
14. Moldova (Gagauz)
15. Moldova (Transdniestr)
16. Nakhichevan
17. Russia
18. Serbia-Albania (Kosovo)
19. Slovenia
20. Spain (Basques)
21. Turkey/Bulgaria
22. Uzbekistan (Kyrgyzstan)

Africa
23. Angola (Cabinda)
24. Cameroon
25. Chad (Aradza); Sudan
26. Comoros
27. Congo
28. Djibouti (Afar)
29. Ethiopia (EPRDF)
30. Ethiopia (Oromo)
31. Ethiopia (Tigray)
32. Ghana (Konkomba, Namumba)
33. Uganda
34. Kenya (Poachers)
35. Kenya (Rift Valley)
36. Lesotho
37. Mali / Niger (Tuareg)
38. Malawi
39. Madagascar
40. Mozambique (Naparamas)
41. Mozambique (RENAMO)
42. Mozambique (UNAMO)
43. Mauritania/Senegal
44. Nigeria (Tiv/Jukun Angoni Ogoni)
45. Senegal (Casamance)
46. Sierra Leone
47. Somalia (SSA)
48. Somalia (North)
49. Tanzania (Zanzibar)
50. Togo

North Africa & Middle East
51. Egypt (Muslims)
52. Lebanon
53. Libya
54. Morocco/Western Sahara
55. Tunisia
56. Iran (Kurds)
57. Iran (Rint Valley)
58. Iraq (Shi'ites)
59. Jordan (Opposition Territories)
60. Yemen

Central & East Asia
61. Afghanistan / Pakistan (Pathans)
62. Bangladesh (Chittagong Hill Tracts)
63. Bangladesh / India
64. Bhutan (Lhotshampas Dragiues)
65. Burma / Thailand
66. Burma (Shan, Mon, Karen, Ka Wa)
67. Cambodia (Reo Komen)
68. China (Tibet)
69. China (Xinjiang)
70. Philippines (Communists)
71. Philippines (Muslims)
72. India (Manipur)
73. India (Punjab)
74. India (Uttar Pradesh)
75. Indonesia (Aceh)
76. Indonesia (East Timor)
77. Indonesia (Irian Jaya)
78. North / South Korea
79. Pakistan (Sindh)
80. Pakistan (Shia)
81. Papua New Guinea (Bougainville)
82. Thailand
83. Thailand and Malaysia
84. Vietnam (Mountain peoples)

Ongoing United Nations Peacekeeping Operations

Mozambique (UNOMOZ)	since 1993
Rwanda (UNOMUR)	since 1993
Somalia (UNOSOM II)	since 1993
Tajikistan (UNOMIT)	since 1993
Eritrea (UNOVER)	since 1992
Yugoslavia (UNPROFOR)	since 1992
Cambodia (UNTAC)	since 1992
South Africa (UNOMSA)	since 1992
Angola (UNAVEM II)	since 1991
El Salvador (ONUSAL)	since 1991
Iraq (UNGCI)	since 1991
Western Sahara (UNMIROS)	since 1991
Kuwait/Iraq (UNIKOM)	since 1991
Lebanon (UNIFIL)	since 1978
Golan Heights (UNDOF)	since 1974

Explanation of Symbols and Definitions

- United Nations Peacekeeping Operation
- Lower Intensity Conflict (minor armed conflict with less than 1,000 deaths per year)
- War (major armed conflict with more than 1,000 deaths per year)

Estimated Number of War Deaths in 1993

Angola	>100,000
Burundi	>100,000
Liberia	>50,000
Zaire	5–20,000
Tajikistan	>10,000
Georgia	>10,000
Azerbaijan/Armenia	>7,000
Somalia	>6,000
Sudan	>6,000
Afghanistan	>5,000
Turkey	>4,000
Bosnia-Herzegovina	>3,500
South Africa	>3,000
Algeria	>3,000
Rwanda	>2,500
Pakistan	>2,000
Guatemala	>2,000
India (Kashmir)	>1,700
Peru	>1,200
Sri Lanka	>1,000
Colombia	>1,000
India (Hindus/Muslims)	>1,000

Estimated Cumulative Number of War Deaths

Afghanistan	1–2,000,000
Cambodia	1–2,000,000
Sudan	1–1.5,000,000
Mozambique	1,000,000
Angola	500,000
Somalia	350,000
Burundi	200–250,000
Bosnia-Herzegovina	200,000
Iraq (Kurds)	180–250,000
Liberia	150,000
Guatemala	150,000
Burma	130,000
Chad	100,000
Colombia	90,000
Sri Lanka	78–100,000
Croatia	50,000
Peru	30,000
Tajikistan	20–50,000
Iraq (Shi'ites)	20–50,000
India (Kashmir)	20–30,000
India (Punjab)	20–25,000
South Africa	20,000
Azerbaijan	20,000

1 THE PROBLEM: TRENDS IN WORLD CONFLICTS

The end of the Cold War, symbolised in the fall of the Berlin Wall in 1989, offered hopes for a 'new world order' based on cooperation rather than fear.[2] These hopes have not been met, despite negotiated settlements to several proxy wars (Namibia, Mozambique, Ethiopia, South Africa, Cambodia). Instead, the Gulf War, the wars in Croatia and Bosnia and the Republics of the former Soviet Union (Armenia-Azerbaijan, Tadzhikistan, Georgia), the continuation of long-running wars in Asia (Sri Lanka, Afghanistan, Kashmir, Burma and East Timor) and in Africa (Angola, Sudan), and the outbreak of new wars (Liberia, Somalia, Burundi, Rwanda), have ushered in a new period of regional instability, global fragmentation, and deepening poverty. The policies and activities of development agencies need to be re-appraised in the light of continuing and probably increasing levels of political violence.

Aggregate statistics on armed conflicts reveal some disturbing trends in the extent and nature of armed conflicts in the 1990s. While the numbers of wars and exact numbers of casualties are surprisingly still open to interpretation, there is a clear upward trend in both the number of wars and the number of people affected by war. In 1960 there were 10 major wars; by 1992, there were 50, 10 of which had started since 1985 (Gantzel, 1994). Not all wars are on this scale. In 1993, for example, 84 wars causing casualties of less that 1,000, and 60 disputes causing under 100 casualties, were recorded (see map NCO, 1994).[3]

The character of warfare is changing. While primitive weaponry when organised (as in Rwanda) can be devastating, the proliferation of small arms, the use of landmines, and the tactics of modern counter-insurgency operations and low-intensity warfare,[4] such as the clearance of land and manipulation of food supplies, have increased the incidence of civilian casualties. In World War II, 52 per cent of war-related deaths were of civilians; in today's wars, civilian deaths make up 90 per cent of deaths (Summerfield, 1990).

Historically, most wars have been associated with interstate relations and state formation. Today, interstate wars appear to be diminishing while internal, domestic, or intra-state wars are on the increase; with the formation of newly independent states this may change.[5] The increase in 'internal' wars is reflected in a growth in war refugees, from 2.5 million in 1970 to 17.5 million in 1992, with a further 24 million displaced persons (USCR, 1993). Of these, 45 per cent are found in Africa and over 80 per cent are women and children. Unless the conflicts which have produced these refugee flows are contained the number of refugees could rise to 100 million by the year 2000 (Rupesinghe, 1992a).

Most of the current internal wars are taking place in the South. In 1993, of 79 countries experiencing war and political violence recorded by UNDP (1994) in 1993, 65 were in the South.[6]

In Africa, in particular, armed conflict and political instability appear to be on the increase. While the end of the 1980s saw reduction in conflict in South Africa, Namibia, Angola, Mozambique, Morocco, and Ethiopia, and democratic elections in several countries, the 1990s have brought new wars in Liberia, Rwanda, and

Burundi, a return to war in Angola, and the intensification of conflicts in Somalia, Sudan, and Djibouti.

Patterns of refugee flows suggest a changing geography of political instability. Refugee populations have declined in East Asia and Latin America, while political instability in Africa, the Middle East, Eastern Europe, the Caucasus and Central Asia has led to increased refugee flows in those areas (Suhrke, 1993).

Wars are also tending to last longer. The war in Angola, for example, has been running for 19 years; there has been war in Mozambique for 13 years, in Sudan for 10, Somalia 5, Liberia 4, Sri Lanka 14, East Timor 19, Afghanistan 15, and Peru 14 years. For the millions of refugees and displaced persons, and the generations who have grown up in the midst of war, conflict has become the daily reality, and development a process of adaptation to insecurity and a state of permanent crisis (El Bushra and Piza-Lopez, 1994a; Duffield, 1994b).

2 THE IMPACT OF ARMED CONFLICT

Armed conflicts are occurring in some of the poorest areas of the globe, and affect the psychological, social, and material conditions of individuals, communities, and whole nations. In many areas social welfare services have been crippled, productive agricultural areas have been laid to waste, and industry has been destroyed or has collapsed. In the 1990s millions of people in Africa consistently face the threat of famine because of war.

The disastrous conditions created by these conflicts have become labelled as 'complex emergencies'. A complex emergency (a term which emerged in the late 1980s in reference to Africa) has been defined by the UN as a major humanitarian crisis of a multi-causal nature that requires a system-wide response. Complex emergencies are distinguished from so-called 'natural' emergencies. They are protracted political crises, which characteristically involve predatory political organisations which survive on war economies sustained through the violent transfer of assets (Duffield, 1994b). Under these conditions famine, food insecurity, nutritional stress, and vulnerability are not the product of 'simple' demographic, climatic, environmental or economic change, but the result of political victimisation. In 1993 there were 26 UN-designated complex emergencies affecting 59 million people (UN, 1994).

In present-day internal conflicts civilians are not just incidental victims, but the main targets, of violence. Guerrilla and counter-insurgency campaigns take civilian populations as their targets. The dehumanising acts of torture, rape, and mutilation carried out against families, communities, and ethnic groups are attempts to destroy the social fabric of society, and thus the first level of 'coping' mechanisms. The trauma, dislocation, and loss of a sense of community (Macrae et. al.,1993; Nordstrom, 1992), and the destruction of community-level organisations, makes survival and recovery more difficult.

The impact of conflict on individuals is mediated through social, political structures, and personal attributes (Bastian, 1993). War disrupts social security networks provided by households and extended kinship systems. In Rwanda and Bosnia, the manipulation and mobilisation of 'ethnic' identities has hardened differences between groups and destroyed long-standing reciprocal relations. In Somalia, where war has hardened segmentation between clans, the practice of exogamy has been relaxed. This has the effect of disrupting economic relations and increasing inter-clan hostility, insecurity, and therefore vulnerability. Wars disrupt the socialisation of children, and, combined with their exposure to and perhaps involvement in armed combat, can cause trauma and exacerbate tensions between age-groups that create long-term problems for social reconstruction.

Wars transform social relations and cause demographic changes which affect people's economic livelihoods. Forced conscription or killings can mean that households no longer have sufficient labour to carry on productive work; landmines can make farming unviable for years; merchants and markets are often the targets of armies, and trading systems collapse. Households are stripped of assets through looting, destruction or displacement. Coping or survival strategies are disrupted by violence, and the sale of assets by the weak enriches the powerful. The incidence of

HIV increases as a result of widespread sexual violence, with consequences for the livelihoods of families and whole communities. Human rights abuses against civilian populations in war have a direct impact on economies and livelihoods. Human rights and livelihood rights are therefore inter-related.

The different capacities and vulnerabilities of men and women determine their ability to cope with and survive conflicts (El Bushra and Piza-Lopez, 1994b). For example, where women's mobility is culturally constrained they may be less able than men to flee from conflict. Wars usually increase the number of female-headed households, and women often have to fulfil their own and men's responsibilities for family provision. Obtaining resources and credit, difficult in normal times, is likely to become harder for women without a male interlocutor. In Somalia, some women have resorted to marrying gunmen for protection. Conflict exacerbates the trends worldwide towards the 'feminisation of poverty'.

Added to the costs of the destruction of infrastructure, production capacity, communications, markets, and environmental resources, are the social costs to countries of maintaining a war. It is estimated that the direct costs of the wars in Angola and Mozambique were $30 and $15 billion respectively between 1980 and 1989. Military expenditure detracts from expenditure on development. A strong correlation has been made between infant mortality rates and the level of GNP devoted to military expenditure (Zwi and Ugalde, 1989). Protracted civil wars frighten away foreign investors, thereby reducing the possibilities of recovery.

Reconstructing countries and communities after war goes far beyond simply rebuilding infrastructure and economies. The effects of trauma and changing social relations, and the need to absorb demobilised fighters into communities, are long-term problems. Because of the protracted nature of many conflict-created emergencies, the usefulness of making a distinction between long-term and short-term needs has diminished. The maintenance and rehabilitation of households, communities, civil organisations, professional associations, and governmental structures need to begin during war. Reconstruction needs to be informed by an understanding of social relations, so as not to reinforce existing disadvantage or further marginalise vulnerable groups.

While the immediate impact of current wars on already impoverished countries is to deepen poverty and vulnerability, armed conflict, fought with ideological motives, may be a positive agent for change. Civil groups, such as women's organisations, NGOs, and community-based institutions, often emerge in response to armed conflicts and can all be positive forces for change. Groups may take up arms to challenge inequality and injustice, as did the ANC under apartheid, and the Zapatista movement in Mexico. In certain situations war may seem preferable to an unjust peace. During the recent fighting in Rwanda, some agencies argued against calling for a cease-fire on the grounds that this would have prolonged the genocide.

After three UN 'development decades', many of the social and economic development gains in the South are being undermined by a rising tide of political instability and violence. Armed conflict and insecurity are now major causes of persistent poverty, a fact accepted by a growing number of NGOs, donors (Dutch

Government, 1993), and the UN (UNDP, 1994).[7] The lives of millions of people, and the livelihoods, culture and integrity of whole communities of people, are under threat; and the very notion of development is being questioned.

3 UNDERSTANDING CONFLICT

The causes of current armed conflicts are multiple and interconnected. They range from the volition of individuals and groups of actors, to structural inequalities and institutionalised injustice. They include unresolved historic issues of identity and sovereignty, issues of governance and democracy, issues of poverty, uneven development, and environmental change. The causes are both local, and linked to the transformations in international political, economic, and military structures brought about by the ending of the Cold War. These conflicts are about struggles over power and rights to 'ways of life'. They concern issues of material, physical, social, and psychological well-being, as well as justice, empowerment, and participation: all of which are part of the rhetoric of long-term development. Clearly, not all armed conflicts need be protracted or generate complex emergencies. Conflicts might become complex and protracted when the causes and solutions are difficult to discern.

Types of Internal Conflicts

- **Ideological conflicts**: These occur between the state and insurgent movements. Social inequality between classes is a dominant theme.

- **Governance and authority conflicts**: These concern the distribution of power and authority in society. Demands from opposition movements are for changes to the political structure of the regime and over control of resources.

- **Racial conflicts**: These include racial conflicts in the USA and Europe.

- **Environmental conflicts**: These are resource-based conflicts over the control and use and misuse of environmental resources.

- **Identity conflicts**: Here the dominant element is ethnic, religious, tribal or linguistic differences. These can be subdivided into territorial conflicts, ethnic and minority conflicts, religious assertions, and struggles for self-determination. A prime concern of combatants is security and the devolution of power.

Conflicts are not static. Resource wars may become ethnic wars. Ideological conflicts may become identity conflicts. Wars may be waged with several objectives. When it is difficult to specify, these internal conflicts become protracted.

Source: Rupesinghe, 1992b.

Armed conflicts also take different forms. They include high technology battles, as in the Gulf War; wars of attrition between organised forces, as in Bosnia; armies of occupation, as in Palestine or Tibet; internal suppression, as in East Timor, Burma or Iraq; and complex insurgencies involving multiple parties, often of untrained fighters, as in Liberia, Somalia or Sudan. Wars affect different social groups, such as pastoralists and sedentary farmers, women and men, adults and children, boys and girls, in different ways. Although each war is different, it is possible to discern commonalities between them.

One commonality is that war is an organised act of (usually) men and therefore it can be modified by political and economic interventions. In order to identify the necessary forms of intervention that can mitigate suffering or bring a resolution to these conflicts we need to move beyond the immediate symptoms of conflicts to understand their causes, and also their impact upon societies. In understanding the causes and impact of current armed conflicts this paper draws on three analytical approaches, considered in the three following sections.

The first provides a political analysis of conflict, which explains armed conflicts as the result of structural factors at local to global level. Current wars are explained as arising from the process of State development and the outcome of development policies. Central to this line of analysis is the relationship between the State and civil society. Current levels of armed conflict and the protracted nature of these conflicts are explained as a result of a systemic crisis, manifest in global political, economic, and social transformations taking place since the 1980s (Duffield, 1994c). This analytical approach is concerned with political and economic processes of change, and the relationship between 'core' and 'peripheral' areas and groups.

The second analytical approach examines the impact of conflict on society, and we use, as an example, the gender analysis of conflict. This takes a more 'actor-oriented' approach, and suggests that conflict needs to be understood in terms of its differential impact on women and men, across social groups, in terms of their socio-economic and political status. The gender analysis of conflict can serve as a basis for the analysis of the impact of conflict on different groups within society. Gender analysis also helps us to understand how conflict can arise from culturally-determined structures of power within families and communities, and illustrates the need to consider conflict at all levels of society, from the micro to the macro, from the personal to the public.

The third approach is concerned with analysing the process of change itself, and in particular with the velocity and turbulent nature of change and development (ACORD, 1991b). This line of analysis is concerned with the implications for operational NGO programmes of a context of instability.

4 THE POLITICAL ANALYSIS OF CONFLICT

The political analysis of conflict argues that current armed conflicts arise from three sources:

- a 'constitutional' crisis caused by a disjunction between the State and society;

- poverty and degenerative change arising from unequal development;

- a systemic crisis arising from transformations in international political, economic, and military structures.

4.1 State-society conflicts

4.1.1 The colonial and Cold War legacies

The current conflicts afflicting Africa are argued by some to arise from the 'original sin' of colonialism and 'incomplete nation-building' (Deng and Zartman, 1991). In Africa, colonisation established a new political and economic order, which included the creation of borders where none existed before, and the imposition of centralised structures of government onto a variety of indigenous political systems. The African states that emerged from colonial rule after World War II inherited boundaries and political systems that had little to do with the cultural and political groupings within their borders. The European model of a unified sovereign nation state, with clearly defined physical boundaries which set the limits of its jurisdiction, was adopted by African states at independence and affirmed by the Charter of the Organisation of African Unity (OAU) in 1964.[8]

During decolonisation the heterogeneity within African states was subsumed in single parties or movements in a common struggle against the colonisers. The liberation struggles legitimised anti-statist politics; and some post-colonial states have experienced continued armed struggles between those who won and lost out at independence. The colonial borders, often arbitrary and poorly defined, have also remained a persistent source of disputes between African states. During the Cold War these intra- and inter-state conflicts provided bargaining chips in regional and international political struggles, thus blurring the distinction between internal and inter-state wars.

Cold War ideologies of nation-building provided the means to suppress discontent. In the aftermath of the Cold War definitions of sovereignty are being challenged and states are under pressure to adapt. With no strategic interests in maintaining particular power structures, the North is disengaging from Africa and pressurising African governments to enact democratic and liberal economic reforms. The weakening of imposed ideological models, and of the mechanisms of suppression, has re-awakened latent ethnic and nationality struggles within states, creating new demands for self-determination (Rupesinghe, 1992b). Deprived, at the same time, of external largesse, those elites who have dominated since independence have become more repressive in an attempt to retain economic and political power. Within this framework, internal wars are seen as a struggle over political power in which the State is a focal point of competition (Rupesinghe, 1989). If colonisation initially fostered a process of State formation, the current internal conflicts are involved in deconstructing the State.

4.1.2 The 'defective State'

Africa's internal conflicts have been linked to the inchoate nature of African states, and the absence of political structures which could regulate competition and co-operation between different interest groups, or exert control (Zartman, 1985). Colonisation failed not only to create the necessary political institutions for the transition to independence, but sowed many of the seeds of current internal conflicts. In many places colonial racial ideology hardened ethnic divisions and created uneven development patterns between regions, and among ethnic, linguistic, or religious groups.

This legacy may be seen in the empowering of Uganda's northern martial tribes, the construction of Tutsi and Hutu identities, and the north-south division in Sudan. Massacres by the colonisers of Harero pastoralists in Namibia, or of Tutsi in Rwanda, established patterns of political repression that are repeated today. The introduction of weaponry by colonists had a profound impact on political relations within and between tribal and ethnic groups. While some colonial administrations may be credited with establishing structures to manage conflict effectively, elsewhere violence was the main export of European imperialism (Lamphear, 1994).

State formation and the forces of modernisation have broadened and deepened these divisions by concentrating political and economic power at the centre at the expense of the periphery. The weakness and fragility of post-colonial political structures in Africa have allowed the ethnicisation of some states based on patron-client loyalties. For some the State has become a means of security and access to resources. For others it has become an instrument for suppression and exploitation.

Communal loyalty expressed through symbols of nationalism or ethno-regional identity, rather than class, provides the capacity to mobilise political action on a large scale. In the absence of other structures, territorial, linguistic or religious sentiments provide a basis for political security. These ethnic sentiments are often interpreted by the State as security threats, resulting in the bolstering of armed forces, and greater suppression by the centre. As the State strengthens its repressive capabilities, its ability to establish communication and bargaining networks between itself and society declines. In this 'defective' or weak State, conflicts arise from a crisis of governance, and the absence of political structures and strong civil institutions which could mediate or manage conflict.

4.1.3 The 'predatory State'

For many peasants, pastoral communities or urban poor, who live on the margins of society, the State appears illusory. Their views rarely penetrate the capital. Day-to-day they are reliant on their own means of survival, articulated through the household or community in which they live. If the State impacts upon them at all, it may be in a 'predatory' form, through taxation or as a 'cattle-rustling apparatus' (Odhiambo, 1991). The monopolisation of power by a central elite at the expense of the periphery produces a model of the predatory State, where control over the political system provides a means to extract resources from society.

This predatory State is intimately linked to the dominance of the political landscape by the military. Many African governments have come to power with the backing of the military, and in many countries the army is a dominant political force. In 1983, 24 of the 50 African governments were controlled by the military; and between 1960 and 1986 there were 144 military coups (Zwi and Ugalde, 1989). In part, this is a legacy of the colonial era. The model of a nation-state protected by security forces was a colonial import. Colonial powers invested as much in developing African military institutions as in developing political institutions. Military service was a source of education for many of Africa's future leaders.

Although accurate data are difficult to obtain, an examination of the economic performance of African countries reveals the effects of the security sector.[9] Military expenditure reduces expenditure on development, monopolises trained personnel, uses up foreign currency, and lessens the possibilities for equitable wealth distribution. The technocratic bias of the military means that they tend to favour industrialisation rather than agricultural development. The most indebted African countries are those whose military debts form the largest share of their total debt.

The integration of the military establishment in the national economy is well established in several countries. In Sudan, Somalia, and Ethiopia, state control of the economy reached its height under military governments (Markakis, 1994). In Sudan under Nimeiri the creation of special trading enterprises controlled by the military enabled army officers to obtain concessions on farming land, for example, the mechanised schemes in the Nuba Mountains, a factor in the 'ethnic clearances' currently taking place there (African Rights, 1993a). Similar links between the military and trading enterprises existed in Somalia during the Barre regime. In Liberia commercial links exist between Nigerian military officers of ECOMOG and the Nigerian military government.[10] Under such regimes the basis of the conflict between the State and society is as much one of commercial interests as ideology.

4.1.4 Resolving State-society conflicts

This statist or constitutional analysis of conflict focuses on what are essentially conflicts over governance and power as symbolised in the State. Prescriptions for the resolution of these conflicts tend to focus on the creation of institutions or mechanisms to manage conflict between contending political forces.

Internal solutions are sought in a dialogue on new definitions of State and nation, the creation of democratic institutions, constitutions (e.g. federal or confederal models), and electoral processes which enable political competition and co-operation, and laws which protect individual, ethnic, and religious minority rights. The search is for a new compact between society and the State, by promoting new forms of co-operation through civil institutions, and coalitions of civic organisations (trade unions, NGOs, civic forums).

Internationally, solutions are being sought in the creation of new, or the strengthening of existing, regional (OAU) or global (UN) institutions for managing internal conflicts (Boutros-Ghali, 1992). This involves dialogue on the limits of sovereignty, and international codes of conduct for the preservation of the rights of individuals and groups. The idea is to transform the arenas and structures through and about which conflict can take place. This institutional approach recognises that the resolution of armed conflicts must be a political process, involving the building of political institutions and structures that ensure a sense of political and economic participation and security for all citizens (Zartman, 1985; Deng and Zartman, 1991; Rupesinghe, 1989).

The application of these prescriptions to date has been less than promising. For example, the aid-democracy conditionality policies imposed by Northern donors on Africa have not only failed to provide sufficient investment to finance political transitions, but have also failed adequately to address questions of legitimacy and rights. Democratic conditionality confuses legality with legitimacy. Democratic practices are the outcome rather than the cause of political change. Elections can 'legalise' illegitimate regimes. In Somalia, the UN attempted to diffuse the technology of democracy through lavish peace conferences, and the formation of regional and district councils, without properly consulting with people on the legitimacy of those bodies.

In seeking a resolution of political conflicts the emphasis should be less on the promotion of legal institutions and procedures, and more on promoting social consensus on the rules that govern political life (Perez, 1992). Human rights conditionality should focus on the obligations and responsibilities of national governments and the international community to the poor and marginalised, rather than on the current negative definitions of human rights by Northern governments, who seek to limit state power. Strengthening the structures of civil society and empowering the marginal sections of society to influence the functioning of the State may be partof this process. In the context of existing wars, the process of identifying and working with legitimate civil or political structures must start during the conflict.

Implicit behind this model of intra-state conflict is a particular Hobbesian view of human nature as having a propensity for violence, which it is the purpose of the State to keep in check. This understanding of the relationship between the individual and society is not necessarily transferable across cultures (Howell and Willis, 1989). Many conflicts take place on the margins of society, involving issues not directly related to the State. There is a need to understand the causes of these conflicts, and how they may become integrated into State conflicts.

The 'defective State' model does not explain why only a few countries in Africa have been wracked by the levels of violence experienced in Sudan, Angola, Somalia, or Rwanda: if the cause of conflict is a weak State, unable to exercise control, or constrained by lack of resources, then one might expect to see more conflict in Africa. Somaliland, for example, a virtually non-existent state, unrecognised beyond its borders, with no coercive powers at its disposal, is currently experiencing less conflict than many countries. Somaliland's advantage may be the weakness of the State, and the strength of its civil institutions. Political solutions to these conflicts may lie less in restructuring the institutions of government, than in separating the idea of the State from the idea of the nation, and re-examining the relationship between the State and society.

4.2.1 Poverty and conflict

Many of the current conflicts are occurring in some of the poorest and most risk-prone areas of the globe, and poverty and underdevelopment are often given as explanations for conflicts. While the 1960s and 1970s saw significant improvements in GNP, life expectancy, infant mortality, and food production, in many developing countries, income disparities between the richest 20 per cent and the poorest sections of the world's population doubled in the same period (UNDP, 1992). The 1980s saw the number of absolute poor in Africa increase, and Africa's share of global GNP decline. The effects of Africa's marginalisation in the global economy are felt in the impoverishment of Africa's semi-subsistence economies.

In pursuit of economic growth, Africa's reliance on the export of traditional primary products has involved the capitalisation of agriculture and the integration of agrarian communities into the market economy. The process has transformed familial relations and the reciprocal and co-operative networks that are integral to the subsistence economy. It has been argued that societies are at their most vulnerable in this transition from a 'moral economy' to a market economy; where traditional systems of social security have not been replaced with institutional insurance, or welfare systems (Sen, 1986). Coupled with high population growth and a decline in the price of primary products,the commercialisation of subsistence agriculture in Africa has led to erratic food production and increased food insecurity. In the 1980s Africa became the biggest recipient of food aid. The pressures of commercialisation on the semi-subsistence economy have upset the balance between economic modes of production and the environment, contributing to a shrinking of Africa's resource base and the growth of local resource conflicts (Twose, 1991).

4.2.2 Development wars

In itself, poverty is not a necessary condition for armed conflict; the poor rarely have the resources to mobilise and revolt. Some of the poorest countries in Africa (Tanzania, for example) have not experienced war. Equally, poverty alone does not explain why Yugoslavia has imploded, rather than poorer Eastern European states. An alternative explanation would be to see poverty itself as an act of 'structural violence' (Galtung, 1990), a manifestation of structural inequalities and the unequal distribution of power, from which armed conflict is one possible outcome. While one might look to the *process* of impoverishment and the structural causes of poverty as a source of armed conflict, wars are not simply the result of political and economic processes, but are deliberately organised.

Injustice, exploitation, and the denial of human rights provide a fertile ground for violence. Human rights issues, such as land rights, are often latent in the design and implementation of many development projects. However, many development projects ignore the political dimensions of development and this, perhaps more than any other factor, has been responsible for the failures of development policies to benefit the poor (Chambers, 1983). A development model that ignores power differentials or heightens social and economic disparities needs to be re-examined. Sustaining such a model sustains endemic violence.

Current development policies and practices have their origins in the particular development models formulated after World War II. The Bretton Woods Conference of 1945, at which the World Bank and the International Monetary Fund (IMF) were set up, established a prescriptive model of global development. It was posited that economic development could be induced in the 'primitive' economies of the 'under-developed' world by applying Western technical skills and economic theory, managed by international institutions (Rondinelli, 1993). When US President Truman declared the Southern hemisphere to be 'underdeveloped' a modernist paradigm was created which contrasted a 'developed' North America and Western Europe with the poverty of the underdeveloped Third World (Sachs, 1993). It provided 'facts' and a 'regime of truth' by which the Third World was known and could be managed.

While it has been argued that the overall aim of post-war development has been the alleviation of mass poverty, it is questionable whether this has been the sole rationale behind development policies (Kitching, 1990). Development has always been imbued with an ideological content; wars have been fought in the name of development. Official development assistance has always involved more than altruism, and been dictated by security and economic interests rather than the poverty of developing countries (Sachs, 1993; Schrijvers, 1993). At the beginning of the Cold War there was a concern in the West that poverty would facilitate the spread of communism and pose a threat to political stability. A view of development aid as apolitical is deceptive and belies the reality of history.

Modernist thinking continues to shape a perception of history as a linear progression from a condition of underdevelopment to one of liberal, democratic, industrial development. However, the progress, peace, and justice promised by modernity has not been forthcoming (Norgaard, 1994). The South, in particular, shows the other side of development: 'growing unemployment, ecological destruction, corruption, heavy drug trafficking, crime, civil war, trade in women and children, increasing numbers of asylum seekers and refugees' (Schrijvers cited in NCO, 1994). Technological development may enable greater control over nature, but it can also deplete resources. The 'Green Revolution' in agriculture has increased production, but it has also increased unemployment and landlessness, and created the conditions for violence (Shiva, 1991). The Kakomba–Degomba violence in Ghana may be partly the result of the capitalist development of rice production in the 1970s. The Zapatista uprising in Mexico may be a consequence of Mexican rural development policies, which in themselves were determined by US economic policies (Redclift, 1984). Development conceived in terms of general social advancement and rising living standards is not a costless process: development can hurt.

Economic development does not necessarily bring about a reduction in violence. The IMF riots or rising levels of violence in the North should dispel the notion that economic growth creates political stability. The current conflicts in Africa show that a process of development which attempts to accelerate economic growth and social change is conflict-ridden and conflict-producing. In one sense, the wars in Africa, and elsewhere, could be defined as 'development wars' (Miller, 1992). The question may be not whether conflict is an obstacle to development, but whether development, as currently formulated and practised, is an obstacle to peace and stability.

4.3 The political economy of war

The statist analyses of wars does not explain the protracted nature of current conflicts in Africa, and the ability of regimes to survive in conditions that have produced societies in a state of virtually permanent crisis. An alternative framework seeks to explain the persistence of these conflicts through an examination of the political economy of war. It draws links between 'local' and 'internal' wars, the instability of Africa's subsistence economy, and the marginalisation of Africa in the global economy.[11]

4.3.1 The new international order

The upward trend in global conflicts has been linked to a systemic crisis in the global economy arising from a restructuring of social and economic systems in the West in the early 1980s (Duffield, 1990; 1994c). The dismantling of the post-war redistributive State during the Thatcher and Reagan years, in favour of an 'enabling' State that promotes market values, coincided with the evolution of regional trading blocs, in North America, Western Europe, and East Asia. Significantly, this period also saw a massive military re-arming in the West; global military expenditure reached a peak of $993 billion in 1987.

This process of structural reform is, in part, held responsible for precipitating the collapse of the planned economies of Eastern Europe and the end of the Cold War. The acceleration of global political and economic integration which has attended the demise of the planned economies of the East has contributed to a resurgence of ethnic and nationality conflicts rather than peace and stability. Economic regionalisation has involved the marginalisation of non-bloc areas. In Africa this has involved a reverse in economic and social development, a decline in foreign development investment, and the introduction of market reforms and safety-net arrangements, implemented through the World Bank, IMF, and NGOs. The geography of political instability reflects the process of marginalisation, with an upsurge in wars in Africa and Eurasia, and a decline in political tensions in East Asia and Latin America. Violence, it is argued, has become a means of political and economic survival where alternatives are lacking (Duffield, 1994c).

The post-Cold-War period has seen a further disengagement of Europe from Africa as the political rationale for aid to Africa has waned. Despite assurances that assistance to Africa would not diminish in the euphoria of a reconstructed Europe, evidence suggests there has been a significant shift on the part of the North away from development investment to relief assistance for the South (Borton, 1993). In part this has been in support of relief programmes in situations of armed conflict. The provision of relief assistance has become a substitute for foreign policy among Northern countries in Africa.[12]

4.3.2 Local and internal wars

Economic decline and resource depletion do not explain the different levels and patterns of violence experienced in Rwanda, Angola, Somalia, and Mozambique. Conflict in Africa has a cultural and political dimension, rooted in historic political relations between different ethnic and socio-economic groups within African states (Duffield and Prendergast 1993).

Warfare has a long pre-colonial history in Africa (Lamphear, 1994). Under subsistence conditions, anthropologists have argued that feuding and warfare had a political function of regulating relations between groups and enabling them to adjust to demographic, economic, and environmental change (Turton, 1989). The aim of traditional warfare was not to subjugate the enemy completely, but to establish political ascendancy to ensure control of resources. It could also be a means of symbolically delineating the political and cultural boundaries of ethnic identity (Fukui, 1994). Warfare could only play this role as part of a balanced system of reciprocity where it was bounded by rules which conditioned the scale and nature of warfare, and the mechanisms for its resolution. It is the collapse of this balanced reciprocity that has transformed African warfare 'from a means of adaptation to an agent for destruction' (Duffield, 1990). This collapse, it is argued is linked to the introduction of new forms of exchange relations as the semi-subsistence economy has become integrated into market economies; a shrinking resource base; the decay of governance; and the spread of automatic weapons. The process began with the colonial penetration of Africa and has continued ever since.

In post-colonial Africa, the process of state formation has generally involved the consolidation of centralised government. Constitutional judicial law has replaced 'customary' law, traditional lines of authority have been weakened, and responsibility for the settlement of local disputes, for example, over land, have been appropriated by the State. While the means for resolving disputes and conflicts at a local level have been weakened, national governments have proved unable to manage local disputes, except by repressive measures.

This disestablishment of the customary systems of government has taken different forms. Some have been abolished, while others have been absorbed into the state bureaucracy. In Sudan, under British Indirect Rule, inter-tribal conflicts were managed through 'tribal conferences'. When the Native Administration was abolished by Nimeiri in 1971, responsibility for settling inter-tribal disputes was given to provincial councils. As tribal elders were not represented on these councils, the tribes were disenfranchised and disputes went unresolved, leading to more protracted conflicts (Karam, 1980). In Somalia, the British colonial administration formalised the office of lineage elders (*akils*) as 'chiefs' and paid them stipends. Under the military regime of Siad Barre, these elders became appointees of the state and thus part of the ruling party and state bureaucracy (Lewis, 1988). Their customary role as peacemakers therefore became subject to party ideology and political manipulation.

The absorption of agrarian communities into market economies generates wealth for some people and impoverishes others. The 'winners' accumulate land, assets, and power; while the 'losers' (often peasants and pastoralists, and particularly women) are pushed on to unproductive land. In Sudan it is argued that as economic decline took hold in the 1980s, and opportunities for generating wealth diminished, the transfer of assets from the politically weak to the politically strong accelerated, with violence increasingly used as a means of effecting transfer (Duffield, 1994b). In the absence of traditional means of resolving disputes, or democratic structures, the introduction of modern weapons in Africa has provided the means for some groups to extend, or redress, this process. The destructive power of modern weaponry destroys any semblance of balanced reciprocity. As asset transfer has progressed, local conflicts have become integrated into state conflicts. As the survival of these groups is dependent on access to food and sustenance, fighting takes place over the semi-subsistence economy. In the process, the vulnerability of the weak increases and the conditions for famine are created.

4.3.3 The politics of famine and vulnerability

War is probably the single most significant factor explaining the persistence of famine in Africa today. Recent literature linking war and famine has significantly shifted our understanding of famine. Famine is no longer seen as an 'event', and the product of natural causes, but as a 'process' of impoverishment and increasing vulnerability which can lead to starvation. This has added a political dimension to previous economic analyses of food insecurity, vulnerability, and famine.

In a reassessment of Sen's analysis of famines, de Waal (1990) has argued that excess mortality in famines can arise as much from a health crisis due to a changed disease environment, as from a shortage of food. This changed environment results from social disruption as people migrate in search of food or income to preserve their way of life. When survival strategies are disrupted social collapse occurs. Social collapse is associated with the onset of violence; people's strategies for coping do not just break down, but are broken by 'systematic violence'. Under such conditions, vulnerability and poverty arise not so much from climatic or economic change, as from political acts of violence. Conflicts therefore add a political dimension to vulnerability: poor nutritional status and starvation may be the result of political action.

Sen's work on entitlements links famine with poverty. Political vulnerability, however, can affect poor and rich alike. In analysing the causes of famine among the Dinka of Sudan's Bahr el Ghazal region, Keen (1992; 1994) argues that, rather than poverty, it was their 'natural wealth' in livestock that made the Dinka vulnerable to raiding from northern Baggara tribes, who themselves had become impoverished as a result of economic and environmental decline. Cattle raiding deprived the Dinka of their means of resisting adversity. Individuals and families were unable to draw on assistance through reciprocal social ties, partly because of a shortage of cattle, and partly because people proved reluctant to help those who, lacking cattle, were unlikely to return assistance in the future. The vulnerability of the Dinka arose from their political powerlessness; they had been excluded since the mid-1970s from participation in government. The process of political marginalisation and disenfranchisement of the Dinka included the dismantling of the Native Administration by Nimeiri in 1971.

Similar examples of political vulnerability include the Muslims in Bosnia-Herzegovina (Duffield, 1994a), the Bantu, Rahanweyne and Reer Xamr in Somalia, or the Tutsi and Twa and Hutu moderates in Rwanda (African Rights, 1994). Conventional economic or physical definitions of vulnerability neglect its political dimensions. Within vulnerable groups, women tend to be even more politically powerless than men. Added to the check-list of the causes of vulnerability, therefore, must be political disenfranchisement.

4.3.4 War and permanent crises

The ability of people to reduce their vulnerability and survive conditions of extreme stress is well documented in the literature on 'coping strategies' (de Waal, 1989; IFRC, 1994). Under conditions of extreme stress people are not passive, but employ their intimate knowledge of the environment, or political and social relations, to mitigate against disaster. The disadvantage is that the employment of such strategies can involve permanent losses. The sale of physical assets by the poor under conditions of scarcity can enrich the powerful. In Sudan during the famine in Bahr el Ghazal, merchants, often linked to the government and military, stood to gain from the sale and looting of the Dinka's cattle (Keen, 1992).

Asset transfer has become a feature of African wars and has led to an analysis of a 'parallel economy', which fuels these wars (Duffield, 1994b). The existence of an informal, parallel economy, beyond the control of the State, is well established in Africa. For many people it is an essential source of income and is not necessarily linked to violence. However, attempts by those in power to regulate and control this economy in a situation of economic decline generates violence.(Miller, 1981). For example, the criminalisation of *khat* production in Somalia in 1985 introduced an element of violence when the military tried to control the trade. This asset-transfer economy has a regional and international dimension. In the Horn of Africa, especially Sudan and Somalia, it is supported by parallel currency markets linked to remittances from the Middle East. The buoyancy of Somali currency and the exchange markets in Mogadishu during the war indicates the strength of this economy (Drysdale, 1994).

The violent extraction of assets from the politically weak by the powerful has its own logic when it becomes a means for conflicting parties to ensure their political survival. The parallel, asset-transfer economy is extremely destructive of the subsistence economy on which it thrives. In places it has resulted in the virtual annihilation of certain ethnic groups (e.g. Nuba, Mundari, Uduk).[13]

The political analysis of famine and war in Africa, which places armed conflict within a historical process, has important policy implications for aid agencies responding to the emergencies created by these conflicts. A framework that conceives of wars and famines as transitory events misses the point that neither famine or war need be temporary if they offer some advantage to the powerful, likely to gain from the process. It is possible to conceive of a 'permanent emergency', developed (consciously or otherwise) to support the survival of the powerful (Duffield,1994b). Consequently, measures taken to strengthen the coping strategies of the losers with compensatory aid, risk, through the appropriation or taxing of aid, supporting the powerful at the expense of the weak.[14] By treating conflict and famine-related conflict within an apolitical humanitarian framework, aid agencies at best risk doing nothing to address the causes of suffering, and at worst become drawn into supporting the continuance of a state of emergency.

Famine and refugees are the final indicators of a process of political impoverishment. When images of the dead and displaced appear on the TV screens, we are too late. Subsequent actions can legitimise a process that has already taken place. Rather than building mechanisms and institutions to treat these symptoms of war through relief or protection programmes, prior action is needed to preserve the political, economic, and cultural assets that support people's way of life. What is needed more than the protection of victims, is the prevention of victimisation.

4.3.5 Moral survival

This analysis of the political economy of war in Africa links the indigenous and international patterns of development with the rising tide of political violence. Armed conflict is explained as a 'survivalist' reaction to a process of degenerative change. It provides an understanding of how hitherto little-explored elements in these conflicts, such as the parallel economy, contribute to their persistence. It makes clear that wars and war economies are not chaotic but are organised for the well-being of some at the expense of others. In doing so it identifies how international aid can become integrated into the structures that generate and sustain violent conflict. It argues that these armed conflicts are, indeed, complex; and that causes and solutions must be sought in the dynamics of global interdependence, including reform of the international aid system.

The systemic crisis argument needs to be moderated by a consideration of the different ways in which economic or resource factors have an impact on individuals and on society as a whole according to particular historico-cultural factors, and against a background of wars outside Africa. At stake is not just the survival of economies or livelihoods, but cultural identity, status, and political survival. The Sudanese war has been going on since Independence. The overt causes of the conflicts in Mozambique and Angola are rooted not in economic crisis, but in destabilisation fostered by South Africa. Arguably, an economic crisis has more significance in the new regions of instability in Eastern Europe and the Caucasus; but here also conflict is compounded by historical factors which, as seen in Yugoslavia, are centuries old. A deterministic or survivalist explanation alone does not account for the different forms of violence in Rwanda, Somalia, Ethiopia, Mozambique, or Bosnia.

Furthermore, while physical security and economic survival can clearly lead people to support Renamo, Unita, the SPLA or the Somali's warlords (Keen, 1994), political and economic survival need not depend on violence. The anthropologist Mauss (1970) argued that trade can be a powerful incentive for co-operation and maintaining human relationships between groups and individuals. Trading links between northern and southern areas of Sudan are said to have contributed to the reduction of tensions in areas of Western Upper Nile in Sudan (EPAG, 1994). The resumption of trade and opening up of grazing land was an important incentive behind the peace process in Somaliland (Bradbury, 1994b). Is it possible that in times of war, when formal national economies collapse, 'moral' as well as 'predatory' economies can emerge? If so, can aid agencies identify and support such an economy? There are many current examples of civil groups throughout Somalia and Bosnia (and indeed throughout history) who have survived through non-violent stances. These individuals and groups rarely receive any publicity or gain the support of the international community in times of war.

5 GENDER AND CONFLICT[16]

A gender analysis of conflict is essential. Analysis of social relations is generally accepted to be necessary if development interventions are to be successful. Gender analysis in particular has offered an important critique of development programmes. In situations of conflict and war, it is essential to analyse social relations, to understand patterns of power, and the nature of change. Inequalities, injustices, and violence are present in the social relations between men and women in most societies. The social, economic, and political inequalities between women and men not only explain why war affects women and men differently, but also the differential impact of conflict across social groups.

The material, physical, economic, and psychological roles of women are fundamental to the way in which people and communities survive and cope with armed conflict. While armed conflict usually affects women adversely, it can also create new opportunities for women to voice their own needs and concerns. Focusing on gender relationships facilitates a move from an abstract analysis of conflict to a consideration of the individual fears and needs of people caught up in armed conflict. It makes the connections between the impacts of conflict on the personal, private, and public spheres of people.

5.1 The personal sphere

Armed conflict exposes everyone to personal risk, whether civilians or combatants, poor or wealthy. Exposure to risk is to some extent gender-differentiated, and varies in different cultures. Women are extremely vulnerable to violence in a world where men still retain a monopoly on the institutions of power and the technology of violence. Although men are liable to be conscripted for combat, and thus to become military targets, women may be less mobile than men and physically unable to escape the fighting. In Somalia, women in general were able to travel more easily than men between clan territories. However, they were also more vulnerable to sexual violence. This threat of violence can constrain women's mobility and affect their economic roles, with consequences for household food security.

In different cultures, structures of gender roles and power relationships determine women's use and control of resources; and their social status and their ability to act in public affects their vulnerability during times of war. Where women are isolated within the family unit, they may have less access to support from external social networks. Single women, women who have been disowned because of rape, or women who have lost their families, may lose those social networks altogether and therefore be at greater risk.

As well as individual trauma, injury, and impoverishment that women may suffer in war, they may also be affected by the long-term consequences of war, in different ways from men. In gathering water and fuel, women may be more exposed to landmine injuries. As a result of their vulnerability and insecurity, women may be forced into marriage. After war has ended, women may be subject to violence by demobilised fighters, who themselves have been psychologically disturbed by conflict.

The forms of sexual violence to which women are subjected mean that women have particular medical, psychological, and material needs. Personal self-esteem and identity are linked to cultural values and roles placed on individuals in society, as well as personal traits. The upheaval caused by warfare may change women's roles and thus their sense of identity and feelings of self-worth. Loss of a sense of self-worth, of identity and value, can inhibit women's recovery from trauma and prevent them from exercising their rights as individuals and members of society. Women and men have been shown to deal with trauma in different ways as a result of their different gender roles and identities. The social stigma associated with sexual violence may mean that women are in need of individual assistance within a community approach to counselling.

More positively, social disruption in conflict can provide opportunities to challenge assumptions about gender norms. Women's active participation in political struggles can challenge gender stereotypes in positive ways.

5.2 The private sphere

For the majority of women, the family is the principle arena of responsibility. During armed conflict, the family unit is often deliberately targeted, and harm to the integrity of the household can affect the well-being of women. In addition, the suffering of other family members can also have an impact on women.

Conflict can leave women shouldering increased responsibilities. Women may be required to take over tasks previously carried out by men. Such an increase in work can have a detrimental impact on women's health. In cases of extreme necessity women may be forced into socially unacceptable activities, such as prostitution or crime, which can leave them ostracised by other family members. Although women may be required to take on new economic responsibilities, their control over economic resources may not increase to meet those obligations. The loss of male family members can threaten women's claims to resources. Women may be forced to sell off their own assets, such as animals and jewellery, in order to survive, which will affect their own future livelihoods. Many such 'coping strategies' involve sacrifices on the part of women.

On the other hand, significant advances in women's position have often taken place when communities face crisis during war or famine. Changes in the household and community sexual division of labour as a result of conflict can be a source of empowerment, as women learn new skills and gain confidence, public respect, and status. All too often, such gains are lost in post-conflict readjustment. Whether those advances can be maintained, and channelled in positive directions, or are lost in the process of recovery and reversion to old ways of doing things, are challenges that face women, communities, governments, and civil organisations in post-conflict situations.

5.3 The public sphere

In the public sphere there are a range of related macro and micro issues concerning women. In times of war, women's cultural roles may be used to reinforce and reconstruct ethnic identities. Cultural perceptions of the vulnerability of women can mean that women are the targets of sexual violence, as a means of symbolically disempowering whole communities. Ethnic and religious fundamentalism may increase restrictions on women's rights by enforcing strict codes of dress and mobility. The same gender bias may mean that women are denied resources which are vital for their own and their family's survival and recovery. While community structures can provide support and protection for women in war, women's specific needs are often neglected. Women's needs may be concealed behind a facade of 'community' needs, as represented and interpreted by men.

The lack of protection of and respect for women's rights remains a serious omission in international responses to wars. The UN has so far failed to condemn the atrocities against women in Bosnia in concrete terms, even less so in Somalia, Mozambique, Rwanda, and other war zones. Underlying the failure to address this subject is a failure by governments, the UN, and NGOs alike, to deal with domestic violence against women, which is a permanent feature of many societies at 'peace'. The violence against women in wars has only brought into the public sphere endemic violence against women in most societies.

5.4 Conflict and power

The impact of armed conflict on gender relations differs between different societies. At best a fundamental change in gender relations may take place; at worst they may harden, or simply be rearranged. Opportunities for change exist, and recovery provides a critical threshold where the action of agencies, civil groups and the state may be able to affect gender relations positively. Women's work as peace and human rights activists is well documented in the North but less so in the South. In Somaliland women had a critical role in seizing the initiative at a critical moment and lobbying for peace. It is important to document these matters. Not only do they highlight the critical contribution women can make in reducing tensions in conflict, but also the real potential for people to resist the inevitable, survivalist trends of war.

The inequalities between men and women exemplify the imbalances of power that lie behind conflict. Gender analysis therefore provides an analysis of war as an expression of the exercise of power. Rape physically and symbolically exemplifies the exercise of power by the powerful over the powerless. The challenge in development and in responding to situations of armed conflict is to create conditions in which imbalances of power and domination of one gender, ethnic or socio-economic group by another do not occur. By pro-actively supporting women's rights, development agencies have indicated that 'solidarity', instead of 'neutrality', is a real option in development, though success has so far been limited.

6 THE TURBULENCE OF CHANGE

In a cursory review of current development literature, 'change' and 'process' appear as key words. Although, arguably, development theory has shifted some way from modernist ideas of linear progress towards a more specific, locational understanding of underdevelopment, much of the language of developmentalism still views development as a linear sequence of change, from 'under-developed' to 'development', from 'vulnerability' to 'sustainability', from 'relief' to 'development'. In this normative framework armed conflict appears, if it at all, as an abnormal, dysfunctional, and temporary event.

A view of conflict as an unusual event in the smooth and slow progress of states and communities towards 'development' proves to be of little use in understanding and responding to the growing number of wars. Furthermore, this view obscures the role that conflict plays in the process of development, and the nature of war itself as a process. It does not help in understanding the complexity and velocity of change, or turbulence, that occurs with the onset of violence. Development is not necessarily linear, not necessarily slow or gradual. The outbreak of conflict can rapidly undermine any semblance of progress. Models developed to deal with 'natural' disasters are ill-suited to dealing with systemic crisis and political fragmentation. Treating conflicts and the complex emergencies they generate as short-term problems, shows a failure to appreciate the nature of the current wars, which have proved to be durable, and more pervasive in their destruction of people, communities, and infrastructure than natural disasters.

War creates a new social reality for those affected by it and for agencies responding to it. In war unpredictability and crisis become facts of life both for those 'being developed' and for those 'doing development'. Agencies can no longer continue to respond to sudden crises in the traditional way, by ignoring them or reacting after the event. The old distinctions between relief and development which this view encourages hinders one's ability to help poor people to cope with turbulent change. If conflict is to be incorporated into developmental or relief policies there may be a need for 'a more refined analysis of what change is' (ACORD, 1991b).

Recognising uncertainty has implications for development planning. The transitions between emergency, rehabilitation, and development are not neat and tidy. Not everything is knowable beforehand. Programming must be open to future uncertainties, future opportunities, and the possibility of future conflict. There is a need to be open to learning and multiple perspectives. Programming in project-sized packages, ignores the non-projectised realities around them. Over-planning of development and relief programmes can result in wastage, when situations suddenly change. Large operational structures and bureaucracies are often the first victims of conflict.

Accepting that development is a turbulent and often conflict-producing process, implies a need to strengthen people's capacities to cope with and survive future shocks and crises. In the same way that gender analysis has become mandatory for many agencies, conflict analysis may also need to become an integral part of assessment, design, and monitoring. Many of the principles of strategic long-term programming, such as participation, the employment of local knowledge, resources, and management capacities, cannot be ignored when responding to short-term needs. Conversely, dogmatically ignoring short-term needs can compound long-term problems. Countries where governments have integrated relief, rehabilitation, and development have had the most success in alleviating hunger (Dreze and Sen, 1989).

Conflicts are not the result of single factors. Responding to situations of armed conflict may require an understanding of the linkages between individual actions; economic, political, and ecological change; and the ability to absorb new information and confront new realities. It requires an awareness of how conflict might be used by some people to further their own ends, and of their sources of support. It requires external agencies to be aware of how their own contributions may compound or create conflict. Because most people survive disaster through their own efforts, rather than those of humanitarian agencies, external interventions need to be planned to take account of local capacities, as well as vulnerabilities (Bastian, 1993). Identifying those variables leads to an understanding of conflict as a process of change with multiple actors, and with 'critical thresholds' or 'windows of opportunity' for interventions.

Figure 1 presents a theoretical model of conflict as a process, and provides a possible programming tool (El Bushra and Piza-Lopez, 1994a). It illustrates how certain points in the evolution of a conflict may represent 'critical thresholds' at which interventions may lead either to peaceful outcomes, or a descent into conflict. In Bosnia, Somalia, and Rwanda, the failure of the UN and regional governments to take advantage of certain 'windows of opportunity' allowed the conflicts there to degenerate and become more protracted (Slim and Visman, 1994). If it is possible to identify these critical thresholds in advance, governments, UN agencies, and NGOs may be able to intervene on different levels to prevent or mitigate the impact of wars. Advocacy on human rights, support for land-right claims, or the resolution of resource-use disputes, for example, might present windows of opportunity for affecting conflict. NGOs and others need to develop an awareness that their own activities can increase local tensions; and that they are themselves part of the process of change, and can therefore influence that change.

6.1 Different perceptions of change

The imperious rationality of much development planning, project appraisal, and emergency programming provides a rarefied language that legitimises actions and political decisions. The designation of something as 'development' or 'emergency' can signal the release and allocation of resources. In an exceptional review of a settlement project for the Giriama in Kenya, Porter et. al. (1991), argue that the 'control-oriented' measures of project planning contrasts starkly with the Giriama's own strategies for dealing with uncertainty in their divination rituals. The Giriama's ability to combine both the physical and spiritual elements of their world to minimise uncertainty proved to have some advantages over the exclusive rituals of the development workers, who offer few alternatives to their linear cause and effect development models; Giriama philosophy is more certain.

Fig. 1 Conflict as a process

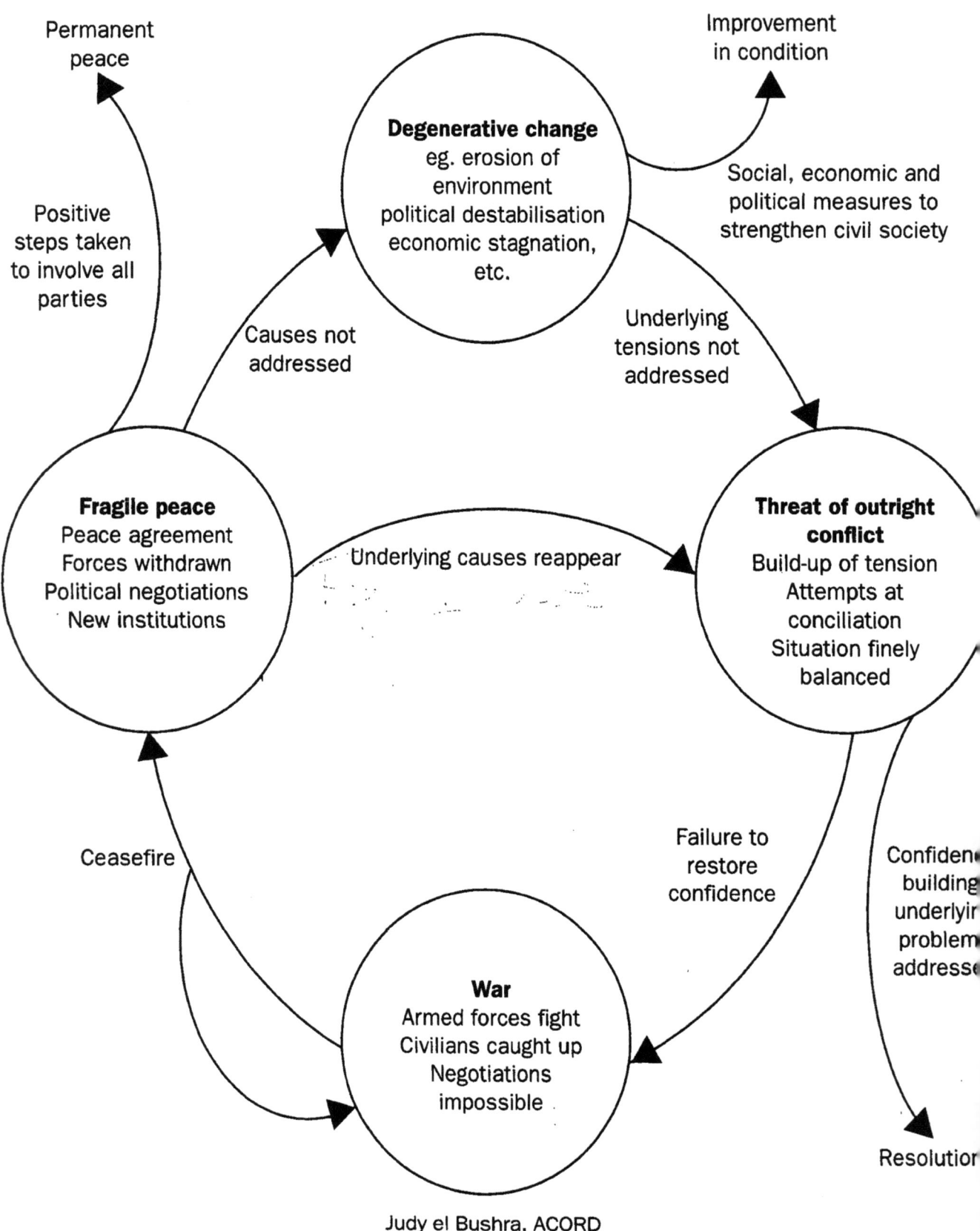

Permanent peace

Positive steps taken to involve all parties

Improvement in condition

Degenerative change
eg. erosion of environment
political destabilisation
economic stagnation, etc.

Social, economic and political measures to strengthen civil society

Causes not addressed

Underlying tensions not addressed

Fragile peace
Peace agreement
Forces withdrawn
Political negotiations
New institutions

Underlying causes reappear

Threat of outright conflict
Build-up of tension
Attempts at conciliation
Situation finely balanced

Ceasefire

Failure to restore confidence

Confidence building underlying problem addressed

War
Armed forces fight
Civilians caught up
Negotiations impossible

Resolution

Judy el Bushra, ACORD

Key Concepts:
Critical thresholds: critical moments when a situation is poised to move in either a positive or negative direction, and when it is susceptible to influence.

Stabilising points: elements within a situation (e.g. people, physical resources, institutions etc. which tend towards stability.

The application of metaphors of chaos and turbulence to the development environment helps to redefine that environment and to reappraise development policy in the light of the current prevalence of armed conflict. However, there may be a danger with imposing, yet again, Western concepts of time and change on to non-Western cultures. In Somalia a new term, neither complex emergency nor turbulence, has been coined to describe the situation there: the word, *burbur*, means 'complete pulverisation'. It refers to a constellation of crises and the depletion of the material, moral and intellectual resources of Somalia (Samatar, 1994). If one were to use 'complete pulverisation' to describe what we now call complex emergencies or turbulent environments, would this produce different policy formulations? The question is whether adding other words like turbulence to the dictionary of development terms, brings development and relief organisations any closer to understanding the actual perceptions and the day-to-day decisions of those affected by conflict? Do participatory methodologies of analysis have something to offer in this respect?

7 RESPONDING TO CONFLICT

War is not a new phenomenon to humanitarian agencies. The ICRC and some of the oldest NGOs, such as Save the Children, Oxfam, and more recent creations, such as Médecin sans Frontières, Médecin du Monde, Health Unlimited, and Concern, were all born from a response to historic situations of armed conflict. As governments and social services collapse under the weight of armed conflict, the formation of civil organisations, such as NGOs, appears to be an inevitable response in many societies; in Europe in the last three years a wave of new NGOs have emerged in response to the war in former Yugoslavia. In their organisational growth many humanitarian NGOs have moved away from crisis intervention to longer-term development work (Korten, 1990). Perhaps because of an implicit belief that political stability can be achieved through development, conflict as an issue has tended to drop from the agendas of NGOs. It is now clear that armed conflict can no longer be considered an exceptional event or an isolated issue. It is a pervasive element on the development landscape, pushing millions of people into abject poverty, and causing severe social trauma, political dislocation, and environmental damage. Conflict in the form of complex emergencies has forced its way back on to the agenda of those humanitarian organisations working for justice and the alleviation of poverty. As the nature of emergencies has changed so too has the nature of external intervention.

7.1 Aiding conflicts

The United Nations, governments, and NGOs are spending vast resources in mitigating the impacts of current wars. Since the 1980s, parallel to processes of economic reform and the rolling back of state structures, there has been a shift in the international aid system away from development investment towards relief assistance (Borton, 1993). Short-term relief assistance, it is argued, is becoming institutionalised as the main response of the international community to situations of armed conflict. Many NGOs, once radical movers in development, have expanded on the back of these conflicts and may be becoming accommodated to them.

This process of institutionalisation can be traced back to the 1970s and 1980s and the phenomenal growth of humanitarian NGOs in response to emergencies generated by conflicts, mainly in the Horn of Africa. The Biafran war in 1968-70, when several medical volunteers criticised the Nigerian government, established a precedent for NGOs operating within countries without the authorisation of the state (Finucane, 1993). In the mid-1980s, during the wars and famines in the Horn of Africa, NGOs, under the banner of neutrality and humanitarianism, crossed borders and reached places the UN could not, constrained as it was by Cold War politics from intervening politically. The cross-border operations in Eritrea and Tigray are celebrated examples of this (Duffield and Prendergast, 1993). In these operations NGOs covertly provided a channel for donor funds into rebel areas. This set a pattern for a division of labour that has subsequently become formalised in sub-contracting relations between the UN, donor governments, and NGOs. ·

The Gulf War and subsequent crisis in Kurdistan caused a further change in the international relief system, in two respects. Firstly, attempts have been made in the UN to strengthen its humanitarian wing, through the creation of a Department of Humanitarian Affairs (DHA) to co-ordinate relief operations. Several government donors, including the British ODA and the EU, have also created their own emergency teams. Secondly, parallel to this, the UN has expanded its peacekeeping role. Of the 29 peacekeeping operations launched by the UN since 1948, 16 have been initiated since 1988. Between 1991 and 1992 the UN bill for peacekeeping rose from $600 million to $2.8 billion and was projected to reach $4.3 billion in 1993 (UN, 1993).[17]

The expansion of UN peacekeeping forms part of the UN Secretary-General's current vision of the UN's policing role in the new world order (Boutros-Ghali, 1992). Originally not provided for in the UN Charter, peacekeeping emerged early on in the Cold War as a safety-valve to prevent regional conflicts from escalating into East-West global confrontations. Since the military intervention in Kurdistan, UN peacekeeping has become a global growth industry, and has changed from merely observing cease-fires to more complex tasks of relief, rehabilitation, and development. What some have termed 'military humanitarianism' has arisen, characterised by the creation of 'safe havens', the erosion of national sovereignty to protect human rights, and the enforcement of economic sanctions. While the precedent for UN peacekeepers to take on non-military duties stretches back to the 1960 Congo crisis, what is particular about the current period is the interweaving of civilian humanitarian operations, through the UN, bilateral agencies, and NGOs, with military protection.

For some who insist on, as yet undefined, universal values of humanitarianism, the growth of military involvement in humanitarian relief operations represents a positive step in meeting the challenges of providing aid and protecting rights in increasingly dangerous environments (Weiss and Minear, 1993). For others it highlights some disturbing trends where aid, foreign policy, and defence are integrated in the same agenda (ActionAid et. al., 1994), and raises the spectre of a new form of colonialism (Pilger, 1993). For example, a recent document produced by the Dutch government envisages strengthening its emergency capacity by integrating the Ministries of Foreign Affairs, Defence, and Development Co-operation (Dutch Government, 1993). The deployment of British and US troops in Rwanda to undertake humanitarian work, rather than peacekeeping, provides further evidence that relief assistance has become the North's principal means of political crisis management in the South.

Concern at the growing military involvement in humanitarian aid is pitched at several levels. Firstly, the costs of peacekeeping or peace-enforcement operations are enormous. In Somalia, for every $10 spent by the UN on military operations, $1 was spent on humanitarian work. There is a real concern that expenditure on military operations diverts resources from non-emergency development investment. Clearly, peacekeeping has benefits for those military establishments which are searching for new roles after the Cold War.

Secondly, there is concern that the merging of aid and foreign policy will mean that decisions on humanitarian aid and human rights are increasingly dictated by geopolitical considerations rather than human need. The high media profile that military interventions receive turns a conflict into an event. The sound-bites of 'chaos' and 'anarchy' provide simple and digestible explanations that reinforce 'natural disaster' images (Lewis, 1993). The causes of the conflict become confused with international geopolitical agendas. One consequence is the increased targeting of aid workers by combatants.

Thirdly, an acceptance of military humanitarianism represents a further institutional accommodation by the North to the political crises and conflict in the South that involves measures which help to sustain these crises. As seen in Somalia, humanitarian objectives can become easily lost in the bureaucracy of military organisation, as security considerations for UN forces take precedence over humanitarian needs (African Rights, 1993b; Bradbury, 1994b). Military intervention reduces aid to a technical fix, and detracts from a search for long-term solutions. Negotiated access programmes, while retaining an aura of neutrality, legitimise the military protagonists in the conflict. The manipulation of relief supplies by military factions, or payments made by the UN to those factions, help to sustain the war economy and weaken alternative civil structures. This may prolong the war by taking responsibility away from local leaders and undermining local reconciliation processes.

Finally, while a humanitarian imperative to protect rights may be the stimulus behind military intervention, it is increasingly clear that military peacekeeping operations themselves can become corrupted and be corrupting. Although human rights abuses often play a critical part in fuelling armed conflict, human rights are given a low priority by UN officials who oversee field operations. The down-grading of human rights is a casualty of 'misguided neutrality', where UN officials seek to establish impartiality in their roles as mediators (Human Rights Watch, 1993). In Bosnia and Somalia human rights abuses, war profiteering, and the encouragement of prostitution, by UN peacekeeping forces is well documented (African Rights, 1993c; Ashdown, 1994). Far from protecting rights and reducing conflict, peacekeeping operations can become a new source of conflict.

7.2 Beyond the relief model

While much has been made of the paradigm shifts in development practice from technology-centred to people-centred, and from blueprint to process development (Chambers, 1993), most NGO emergency relief programmes remain externally managed, non-participatory, and heavily dependent on expatriate staff. Relief aid is delivered to those in need, as defined by the implementing agencies. As communities turn into 'vulnerable groups', the emphasis is on 'intervention in' a situation, rather than 'working with' people. The emphasis on the modalities of control helps agencies to ensure neutrality. The aura of neutrality and charitable altruism is reinforced by the fundraising images of humanitarian relief organisations. The typical iconography of the child refugee plays on Western ethnocentric notions of childhood and reinforces a perception of 'vulnerable dependency' (Gibbs, 1994).

A consequence of externally-managed, technically-orientated relief programmes is that agencies often fail to recognise local resources and skills (particularly those of women), and miss the opportunity for involving local communities in the management of relief (Slim and Mitchell, 1992). At the same time the new

34

bureaucracies, such as logistical units and refugee commissions, that are created, may have their own interest in maintaining a dependent constituency (Harrell-Bond, 1993). The channelling by donors of resources through NGOs shifts accountability and responsibility away from national governments, local leaders or communities, thus undermining local capacity and creating further dependency. Relief aid often creates tensions among local organisations or refugee and host populations over access to external resources. Relief aid can therefore undermine co-operative relations rather strengthen them (Harrell-Bond, 1993).

A historic analysis of development argues that the neutrality of aid is an illusion. Even the most benign forms of development can disturb the *status quo*. Any intervention can potentially affect, positively or negatively, the dynamics of a conflict. The provision of aid through 'neutral' NGOs provides donors with the means to maintain a political distance, while exerting some control over the resources disbursed. Prime examples are Bosnia and Rwanda, where humanitarian aid has become an excuse for the lack of political action by donors. By providing assistance, NGOs themselves become part of that dynamic; by effect or intent they act politically. This has important policy implications for donors and aid agencies responding to the emergencies generated by these conflicts.

Gender analysis indicates that conflict can be a positive catalyst for change. Gender relations may change as social systems are disrupted, with women shouldering added burdens, but gaining increased status and independence at the same time. New civil institutions can emerge to challenge the nature of the state or regime. Opportunities may arise for civil organisations to focus on issues of human rights and economic and political development. Local institutions, women's organisations, and associations of professionals may have a crucial role to play in developing grassroots peace-building. For example, the joint efforts of lineage elders, women's organisations, and traders in Somaliland to restore a fragile peace after four years of war, indicates what is feasible, when the conditions and will are there (Yusuf, 1993; Bradbury, 1994b). Foreign agencies can have a role in helping to create the conditions for such processes to multiply. They will also need to watch for the erosion of women's new-found independence (as is currently happening in Eritrea) and act to support the consolidation of changed gender relations where appropriate. If emergency and humanitarian assistance remains strictly defined in terms of food aid and medical relief, it runs the risk of undermining local production systems and local capabilities. This in turn can lead to a weaker civil society and the reinforcement of unpopular and undemocratic government or movements.

Acting on these conditions requires sensitivity, a level of analysis, and a long-term perspective that are often absent from short-term relief operations. It can sometimes require agencies to make political choices. Solidarity with the ANC, or with the TPLF and EPLF, for example, recognises that in some conflicts choices may have to be made. Mediation, whether direct or through aid, may perpetuate war by meeting 'villainy' halfway (Miller, 1992).

8 ORGANISATIONAL ADAPTATION IN CONFLICT SITUATIONS

The following section reviews some of the key issues that development and relief organisations may need to consider in responding to situations of armed conflict. A key theme to emerge from the foregoing analysis is the need to understand conflict as a historical process that is mediated by socio-political and economic structures, at a micro and macro level. It is a process that involves social actors (as individuals and communities), who are differentially affected; there can be winners and losers. One way of considering what organisational adaptations agencies might make is to look at the different stages of conflict progression (Fig 2). The section follows this approach, looking at *Development and conflict, Working with conflict,* and *The problems of peace*; and concludes with some reflections on operational issues, advocacy and policy reform, and the process that organisations might go through in thinking about conflict.

Awareness of conflict

		Low	High	
P o w e r	Balanced		Negotiation	sustainable peace
	Unbalanced	latent conflict	overt confrontation	

Figure 2: The Conflict Progression (From Curle, *Making Peace*, Adaptations, Lederach)

8.1 Development and conflict

8.1.1 Conflict as a strategic development issue

Development is a turbulent process of change, in which environmental decline, political instability, economic crisis, and wars are likely to occur, and re-occur. The long-term impact of wars on the poverty of nations and regions, and the livelihoods and vulnerability of individuals and communities, means that conflict can no longer be left to the purview of government security structures, or the UN Security Council. Conflict has to be incorporated as a strategic issue into the work of agencies working for poverty alleviation and justice.

How can agencies approach conflict as a strategic issue? The first step may be to move away from a perception of armed conflict as an aberration. While the conflagration of internal wars and the emergence of complex emergencies perhaps mark a historic and disturbing shift in global political and economic systems, conflict, from the level of dispute to the level of endemic violence, is a feature of life for many people throughout the world. In 1993, when the UN designated 26 conflict-generated emergencies as 'complex', there were over 80 other violent conflicts recorded (see section 1, *Trends in armed conflict*). In many countries not at war violence and insecurity are daily realities in the private and public lives of many women, children, and ethnic and religious minorities, with profound consequences for their physical, psychological, and material well-being. Insecurity and violence are developmental issues that have received little serious attention from the UN, governmental agencies, and NGOs working for poverty alleviation and justice.

For example, conflict over land or in the form of cattle rustling is a chronic problem for pastoral nomadic and sedentary farming groups in many countries (Lane and Swift, 1989; Oba, 1992; Markakis, 1993). As one writer has noted 'pastoral development is often as much concerned with the management of conflict between competing interests as it is with physical or economic improvements' (Prior, 1994). Development interventions can exacerbate these conflicts. Agricultural or veterinary extension programmes are unlikely to have the intended impact in areas where land tenure is a contentious issue. Supplying inputs to farmers may exacerbate tensions by legitimising disputed occupancy. Emphasis might be better placed on supporting community or government institutions that are in a position to resolve competing claims, before distributing inputs. A study of conflicts between farmers and pastoralists in Senegal demonstrates the ability of communities to manage their own internal conflicts over resources effectively, once the rights of local people and their responsibility for managing the resources were recognised (Gueye, 1994).

A great deal of time is often taken up by government officials in trying to mediate or settle such conflicts. At the same time centralised government bureaucracies, judicial structures, and government staff in many countries are often poorly equipped to deal with such disputes. Few, if any, government employees are trained in mediation and dispute resolution. At worst, national political, economic, and environmental development policies, such as resettlement programmes, land tenure policies, unequal inheritance laws, industrial relations policies; and technological developments, such as dams, water supplies or roads (as in Britain), over which people do not have democratic control, can create the conditions which generate conflict.

Equally, NGO development programmes, with their own hierarchical and alien bureaucracies, where 'development' is implemented in project-sized chunks, and which rarely look beyond the amorphous 'community', or 'target' groups, can create their own forms of turbulence. Few NGO staff are trained in mediation or dispute resolution. Despite the political rhetoric of empowerment strategies, much of community development glosses over conflicts of gender and class, or political issues such as land rights.

The development policies of major donors can also generate conflict and have an impact on the evolution of conflicts. Environmental or structural adjustment policies, for example, can exacerbate divisions between rich and poor and between different resource-users, and thus exacerbate underlying causes of conflict. Conditionality associated with economic liberalisation, the rolling back of the State, and democratisation following Western models, may engender conflicts, and weaken the State's ability to mediate between them. Trade policies designed to promote the commercial interests of manufacturing countries are often directly contrary to the economic and livelihood needs of the poor. This is seen most starkly in the case of the arms trade.

The annual budget of WHO amounts to three hours of the global expenditure on arms. Half a day's global arms expenditure would pay for the immunisation of all the world's children. While Northern governments make aid conditional on good governance, they continue to export to the South the materials (including torture equipment and arms) that support bad governments. The greatest transfer of technology from rich to poor countries is armaments. Ever since the Vietnam War, the South has provided a testing ground for the North's destructive technologies; the export of equipment for manufacturing poison gas to Iraq by Britain is a recent example. The wars in the South reflect the priorities of the world powers, and are one way in which they exert their influence. The duplicity of arms manufacturers being paid by aid donors to advise on the removal of their own landmines is a recent case in point. As Zwi and Ugalde (1989) noted, 'there is little doubt that much of the political violence in the Third World will subside the moment industrial nations cease to export it.'

Questions: How should governmental, inter-governmental agencies, and NGOs address conflict as a developmental issue? Are some forms of development more likely to generate conflict than others? What forms of governmental, inter-governmental structures, or civil organisations are best able to manage or prevent conflict? How should these organisations tackle the problem of the arms trade?

8.1.2 Conflict prevention

If, as suggested (section 6), conflicts can move from latent to overt expressions of violence, this implies that it should be possible to identify 'critical thresholds' and to affect outcomes through political or economic interventions. Certain interventions may increase the likelihood of conflict while others may help to reduce the likelihood or prevent the escalation of conflict.

The international response system, including the UN, governments, and NGOs, is generally geared towards the protection of the victims of conflict only after conflict has developed into full-scale war and pathological violence. Then survival and security become the burning issues, making relief operations or, in extreme cases, military intervention, apparently 'the only option'. Is it possible to prevent or reduce the escalation of wars?

Answers to this question depend partly on an analysis of the causes of conflict. If the current wars are essentially conflicts about power, over the State, or arise from unmet needs, then it may be possible to develop institutional means to prevent or manage such conflicts, and to build democratic structures that ensure participation and equity. If the conflict arises from conditions of poverty, then conflict may be prevented by addressing the structural causes of poverty. However, if the war is being organised for the benefit of some people, to the detriment of others, then military action may be needed to counter this.

The United Nations Secretary-General (Boutros-Ghali, 1992) has set out various options for conflict management in the 'new world order'. He has emphasised the need to develop conflict early-warning systems, and for conflict prevention and preventative diplomacy. Emphasis is placed on strengthening regional organisations such as the OAU and ASEAN in dealing with regional conflicts. To what extent is this new agenda working?

Diplomacy and sanctions: Peace agreements and preventative diplomacy did not prevent genocide in Rwanda. Elections did not prevent the renewal of conflict in Angola. The deployment of a human rights monitor to Sudan has not prevented the continual 'ethnic cleansing' of the Nuba from central Sudan. The regional peacekeeping forces in Liberia have not brought an end to the war there. Democratic elections did not prevent the military from retaining power in Nigeria or seizing power in The Gambia. Continual monitoring and protestations by human rights activists about East Timor have not prevented the sale of arms by Britain to Indonesia.

On the other hand, diplomacy has helped to bring an end to apartheid in Namibia and South Africa, allied to internal pressures for reform and economic and cultural sanctions. Mediation by the San Edigio religious community and regional governments helped to broker a peace agreement in Mozambique (Vines, 1994). International diplomacy has assisted in bringing about the peace agreements in Israel. Dialogue has contributed to the IRA cessation of military operations in Ireland.

Early warning: Until recently, few organisations, except internal security agencies, have monitored potential conflicts. As human rights agencies, such as Amnesty International, Human Rights Watch, and African Rights demonstrate, information is crucial to the protection and promotion of human rights. The electronic information revolution has created new opportunities for monitoring, and for making information the basis for action on conflict prevention and diplomacy. However, few development agencies actively monitor the countries in which they work for potential conflict. Rather than reacting after the event, can relief agencies monitor areas of instability for new conflicts and work to prevent conflict? Could human rights monitoring be incorporated into disaster early-warning systems?

Strengthening civil society: Some analysts view the growth of NGOs in the past decade with unease as it matches a decline in the North of a redistributive and accountable state. Others view the 'third way' of NGOs as a means to strengthen people's participation and control over their own affairs, by ensuring accountability and democratic development (Clark, 1991). Non-governmental civil organisations can play a role in preventing conflict; for example, in India a coalition of civil organisations, film stars, and pop stars helped to prevent an escalation of religious conflict in that country, which the government appeared unable to control.

Recently there have been a number of conferences and networks established to bring together governmental and non-governmental organisations on this issue. International Alert, for example, recently facilitated an international conference in Addis Ababa on 'The Challenge of Peacemaking in Africa', to strengthen conflict resolution capabilities in Africa.

Questions: To what extent do, or could, conflict prevention measures achieve their aims? What kind of information is needed and to whom should the information be sent? What networks exist to put pressure on the right people in the right organisations at the right times? Which are the appropriate organisations to undertake this work?

8.1.3 Conflict analysis and planning

Understanding the impact of development interventions requires a 'process approach' to programme planning which, through monitoring and evaluation, routinely and explicitly questions whether activities will reduce the likelihood of conflict, or risk exacerbating it. To what extent, for example, did support by development agencies for communal work (*umuganda*) in Rwanda contribute to the creation of the *interahamwe* militias that carried out much of the genocidal killings in Rwanda (African Rights, 1994)?

In order to be able to ask such questions and to make political judgments, conflict analysis and human rights issues need to be built into vulnerability profiles, feasibility studies, programme designs, and monitoring and evaluation systems. Political analysis is often missing, or at best only implicit, in development projects. A review of logical planning frameworks on ODA-funded development projects in Asia, for example, revealed only a limited analysis of the political environment in which projects were being implemented, and the political impact of those projects on inter-group relations and relations between people and government (Shepherd, forthcoming).

Certain forms of analysis may reveal latent tensions and the likelihood of future conflicts. For example, a participatory appraisal of a proposed irrigation system in Zimbabwe revealed the fears of women that men would spend any extra income generated on drinking, thus increasing household tensions (Welbourn, 1993). Programmes that seek to reduce vulnerabilities or strengthen capacities may need to adjust activities or incorporate measures to manage or resolve such conflicts before they become protracted. This requires a level of knowledge and trust between an agency and community that can only be built up over time.

In understanding conflicts the importance of historic factors is increasingly recognised (El Bushra and Piza-Lopez, 1994a; Keen, 1994). However, historical analyses are almost entirely missing from the policy and project documents of development agencies. Needs assessments, socio-economic household analyses, and vulnerability profiles of stable communities or refugee populations capture the conditions of people at a particular moment in time, and are usually devoid of any historical perspective. Evaluations rarely cover longer periods than the funding cycle of projects. The few exceptions show the great value of a historical perspective (Porter et. al., 1991).

Questions: What forms of analysis and methodologies are available and most appropriate for analysing the causes and impact of conflicts? And who are the appropriate organisations to carry out the analysis? Do relief and development agencies (both NGOs and official agencies) have the relevant skills and capacities? If not, where can these be obtained? What organisational adaptations are required to make use of the new information? Can conflict analysis and political analysis be incorporated into programme design, where a discussion on ethnic or tribal conflict might be construed as racist or where political dialogue is banned?

8.2 Working in situations of conflict

8.2.1 Development in situations of conflict

The longevity of many armed conflicts suggests there is a need to move away from a simplistic, and by now anachronistic, distinction between development and relief. Long-term development programmes need to be tested against their ability to give people the capacity to deal with crises, while short-term relief activities need to take into account future needs and long-term consequences of their actions.

Work which can be done in the midst of war

Meeting basic needs: This is work to relieve immediate suffering by the provision of basic welfare in the form of food, water, shelter, medical treatment and safety. This might include sheltering refugees and displaced persons, transportation of wounded, tracing and re-uniting families, and burying the dead.

Mediation and negotiation: This is work to facilitate the declaration of cease-fires and safe zones, arrange the transfer of hostages or prisoners, to limit weaponry, target or zones of fighting. This involves meeting combatants, politicians, civil servants, diplomats and working towards direct meetings and negotiation.

Political options: This continues the work of mediation and negotiation and helps to institutionalise a peace process, by helping to formulate laws, treaties, boundaries, constitutions, voting procedures, and other political measures to transform cease-fires into truces and truces into settlements.

Promotion of justice and rights: The protection of rights during war might include monitoring the treatment of civilians, prisoners, and the wounded, and enforcing bans on the use of chemical or biological weapons, torture, and other illegal acts. It includes making people aware of their rights. This might include active use of the media and lobbying of governments and donors.

Development: In the midst of war development work must continue, to ensure there are structures and institutions on which reconstruction can begin. This might include training in primary health care, literacy, sanitation, water, agriculture, veterinary work, and support to civil institutions.

Physical rehabilitation: The rebuilding of some infrastructure, such as roads, water systems, transport, and communication systems, needs to continue during war, not only to ensure the delivery of welfare services, but also to help to keep communities together.

This paper cannot cover all the possible needs and ways of working in situations of war listed above. In working in conflict, NGOs, UN, and donors may need to consider appropriate divisions of labour, based on their particular capabilities, rather than each agency trying to build up skills in all areas. A danger of the division of labour, however, is that it may lead to the further institutionalisation of the aid system, as seen in the NGO-donor sub-contracting relationship. Attempts to improve co-ordination, through the development of the DHA and ECHO, have in many cases created more confusion and wastage than solutions.

A key issue for working in conflict is flexibility. Different weighting may need to be given to different kinds of activities at different points in time. Figure 3 presents the changing emphasis between different programme activities that has been observed in ACORD's programmes, and this diagram can be used in conjunction with Figure 1. Acceptable practices in 'stable' conditions will need to be adapted in conflict situations. For example, standard criteria for credit schemes and cost recovery may be inappropriate in conflict-affected areas. The prevailing economic conditions may be such that any incomes generated, or the loans themselves, are needed for simple survival rather than investment. Schemes designed in a period of crisis must identify from the outset the capacity of the target group to service loans and determine accordingly whether grant or loan-type activities are most appropriate. Rather than continuing credit schemes, and allowing loans to become *de facto* grants, ACORD in Juba in Sudan has switched from the provision of tools and seeds on a credit basis, to pre-payment. The introduction of higher value crops by ACORD made it possible for farmers to pay cash in advance. Just as important as credit is support to savings and loan groups.

Questions: How do relief and development organisations define their roles in conflict situations? How do they decide to respond to one emergency rather than another?

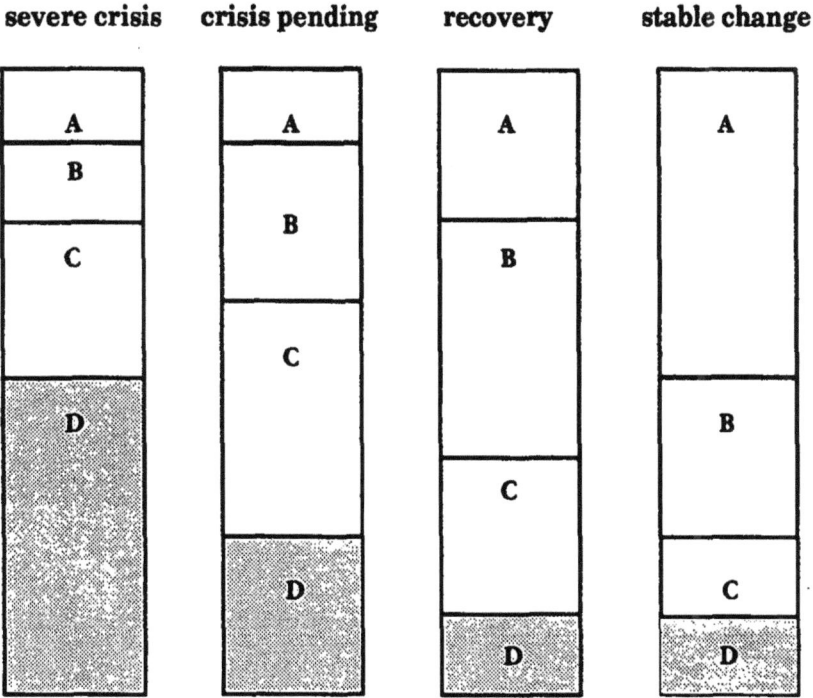

Figure 3 The changing emphasis of support

A represents support needs and roles related to: income-generation, enterprise development, savings and credit, sustainable health and education systems, environmental protection, capacity building, institutional development; encouraging strategic alliances, increasing ability to dialogue with the State and undertake national and international lobbying, preparing withdrawal; reinforcing women's entitlements and rights to gain access to credit, health, education, legal protection; promoting and strengthening women's ability as individuals and as groups, and developing networks and alliances with progressive agencies, legal services etc.

B represents support needs and roles related to: political stability, democracy at all levels, organising capacity, self-confidence, increased ability to deal with next crisis, securing and re-starting production, rehabilitating or establishing infrastructure; broad-based training, network building, strengthening people's ability to place demands on government, building economic foundations for group development; the readjustment and renegotiation of women's roles and gender relations; promoting and strengthening women's groups and women in mixed groups.

C represents support and roles related to: preparedness for possible crises, contingency planning, securing production, diversifying options, strengthening coping mechanisms; consolidating local control and management of resources by credit, training, support for organisational capacity; women as managers and consumers of shrinking resource base, directly involved and supported in all projects.

D represents support needs and roles related to: relief (eg food, shelter, medicine), preservation of local culture, strengthening of local coping mechanisms, political protection and lobbying, securing production; the provision of a liaison between community and external providers; thinking with community, 'being there', moral support, emphasis on life-enhancing principles, and avoiding dependency; women as guardians of family and culture, and as providers; protection, ensuring that although vulnerable, women are not seen as victims.

Source: ACORD, (1992) Operationality in Turbulence.

Case-study 1: New Ways of Working in Conflict Situations

The conflict in Mali during 1991-2 quickly made existing infrastructural work (irrigation and well-digging) impossible. However, by developing new ways of working, the ACORD programme staff were able to continue support for revolving funds and credit schemes, and the provision of small-scale agricultural equipment.

It quickly became too dangerous to use motor vehicles to visit rural communities, or to build up stocks of fuel and spare parts, as these became targets for attack. Initially the teams switched to safer forms of transport (camels, horses, and boats) to service communities, but it then became too dangerous for any sort of movement, and this led to the development of what has been called the 'inverse method'.

As ACORD staff became increasingly restricted to the towns, communities took the initiative in communicating with field staff. They sent written or verbal messages via representatives, traders or fishermen on the Niger, to ACORD about what was happening, what the problems were, and what support was needed. Community representatives, who enjoyed greater security than ACORD staff, travelled to ACORD offices to negotiate forms of support such as funds and small-scale equipment which they could transport easily. The teams used these meetings (and wider inter-community meetings) to monitor activities, decide on the best forms of support, and satisfy themselves that the support reached its intended destination.

ACORD also made use of its drivers and boatmen, who as local people had greater freedom of movement than other members of staff. Using audio tapes to assist the process, they progressively took on a greater role in animating community meetings. Meetings were facilitated on the basis of prompts and notes developed by the teams, and the discussions were taped. The teams then listened to the tapes.

The basis for this development was the institutional development support, and particularly a major auto-evaluation exercise, that had preceded the conflict. As a result communities were better able to analyse their situation and propose solutions and forms of support.

However, there are inherent problems in the 'inverse method'. As it relies on groups or individuals coming to ACORD there are obvious implications both for beneficiary targeting, and the preservation of neutrality. Immature groups, or those for whom ACORD is inaccessible, are at a considerable disadvantage. Future use of the method would need to address these shortcomings.

8.2.2 Strengthening coping strategies

The provision of emergency assistance in a developmental manner might include supporting local coping strategies and assisting local institutions to weather crises, with the aim of improving their ability to survive future crises unaided (ACORD, 1991a). This might involve ensuring that basic needs are met by promoting 'relief production' or 'relief income generation', rather than just the provision of commodities (Case studies 2, 3 and 4.)

Case study 2: The emergency distribution in Gulu, Uganda.

In 1989-1990 ACORD carried out an emergency distribution in Gulu, northern Uganda. Gulu was the site of a long-standing ACORD rural development programme. When fighting broke out between the NRA and rebel groups in 1987, ACORD staff, along with the rural population, were forced into Gulu town.

Within Gulu town, conditions were extremely harsh, with limited relief supplies, and the town's infrastructure was unable to cope. The ACORD Rural Development Workers (RDWs) carried out a needs assessment with those displaced, who expressed the need for tools, seeds, and support so that they could utilise land in the town for food cultivation. This would complement relief supplies from other agencies, and, the programme team believed, limit the growth of a feeling of dependency. A package of goods was jointly identified. It was originally proposed to include machetes, but it was feared that rebels would take them as weapons, and they were replaced by axes.

By the time the funds began to arrive (in mid-1989), people had started to return home, and the team went ahead with the distributions in the rural areas in order to encourage resettlement. The ACORD team implemented the distributions itself, registering people, and transporting and distributing the goods.

Gender issues were addressed by the use of a *kenoor* (cooking fire) as the registration unit. This ensured that women received the tools, though an exception was made for single men, certified as such by the local authorities, who were also registered. This was important in a polygamous society where the women do most of the agricultural work.

Because of the emphasis on self-reliance in the programme's methodology, and uncertainty that programme teams could depart from programme proposals and budgets, the distribution prompted considerable debate. However, it was felt that in conditions where people lacked the basic necessities, a programme could not continue to focus simply on animation and self-reliance, and remain relevant. However, the team did use the programme's 'developmental' and participatory principles in their response, and the distributions enhanced ACORD's reputation and provided an entry point for longer-term work.

A strategy to support local coping mechanisms needs to be approached with caution. Measures to help one group to 'survive' may place additional burdens on others. For example, the movement of people away from war zones in search of security and food creates problems for host populations in terms of competition for resources and environmental degradation. Large-scale relief operations in support of the forced migrants can exacerbate these problems if host populations are not involved and consulted. This is currently happening in Tanzania with the influx of Rwandan refugees. Furthermore, the provision of relief to safe-havens or refugee camps can encourage the migration of people and assist military strategies to depopulate contested areas (Keen, 1992).

Case study 3: Emergency support to agricultural production

ACORD began implementing the Juba Economic Recovery Programme in 1987, after the SPLA had laid siege to the town in southern Sudan. The programme laid out a three-year programme of economic assistance to the population in the form of support for agricultural production and small businesses, and a rehabilitation programme for the displaced.

The agricultural component has provided a Tractor Hire Service (THS), seed, tools, advice, and support to the town's inhabitants. These services have opened up land unused for agriculture for decades, allowing the production of considerable amounts of food. This has helped to counter the development of a mentality of dependence by broadening and supporting coping strategies; it has helped to supplement inadequate and unreliable air-lifts of food aid to the besieged town; and it has proved to be seven times cheaper to grow food than to fly it in. Furthermore, as the security zone around the town has expanded and new areas of land have become available, the programme has been able to offer these services to displaced people.

The movement of refugees, which typically involve more women and children than men, can result in the disruption of the family unit; a loss of assets and resources such as land; and psychological stress. The employment of one survival strategy involves the loss of opportunities to deploy others. Choices are made. The employment of coping strategies, such as the sale of assets, can enrich the powerful, and compensatory aid to shore up coping strategies may reinforce this process. Under stress people are often reluctant to sell off assets needed for future investments (de Waal, 1989), and the sale of food aid may not represent an absence of need or abuse of the system, but attempts to preserve other assets. Agencies should perhaps be acting to ensure that people do not have to resort to such coping strategies in the first place.

Gender analysis reveals the danger of treating communities as undifferentiated wholes. Particular groups in a community (e.g. women or the elderly) have different basic needs and may employ different strategies to survive. On the other hand they may be prevented from doing so due to cultural constraints which can go unrecognised in emergency situations. For example, in Somalia Oxfam distributed clothes to women who, because of loss of clothing, were unable to leave their houses to get food supplies. Support to local coping strategies requires an understanding of local conditions and cultures.

Case study 4: Emergency support to income generation

ACORD's Juba Economic Recovery Plan has suffered considerable problems in attempting to use credit and achieve cost recovery in a conflict situation. In the agricultural component, tractor hire, tools, and seeds were initially provided on a credit basis. However, repayment rates were unacceptably low. Cost recovery has been improved by changing to a system of pre-payment in cash for the tractor hire service, tools and seeds, instead of providing them on credit.

The Small Business Promotion Component (SBPC) also had problems. Two evaluations in 1992 found the programme was failing to reach significant numbers of people, despite the high level of informal trading in the besieged town. The scheme was judged by Juba's inhabitants to be unresponsive and inappropriate, private money-lenders being more responsive and efficient.

A number of problems were identified in the SBPC. Staff losses due to the conflict had left the programme team with insufficient capacity to respond effectively, and a sustained period of training and support was recommended. In addition, research was needed into existing patterns of lending, and how ACORD could make its methodology and procedures more responsive. (For example by decentralising the team and establishing 'neighbourhood offices'.) In addition, this research might reveal other, non-credit methods of supporting and promoting income-generating activities. Training was proposed to strengthen the community's ability to make use of credit.

However, a key survival strategy of people in war is a commitment to group survival. As Ryle's work with the Dinka in Sudan revealed, their concern was not so much with the preservation of life itself, but the preservation of a 'way of life' (Slim and Thompson, 1993). The UN Convention Relating to the Status of Refugees (1951) lays down that the 'maintenance of culture' is a particular right of refugees. However, this can be undermined by the emphasis of humanitarian agencies on the protection of the rights of individuals, when responding to the needs of vulnerable groups. The vulnerability of these individuals (who may be women, the young, the old, or refugees) partly stems from the break-up of households and communities and the targeting of specific minority groups. The Muslims in Bosnia, the Tutsi in Rwanda, the Nuba in Sudan, and Shi'ia in Iraq are vulnerable, not because of their individual status, but because they are members of a particular group. Focusing on community, or group rights, rather than individual rights might focus humanitarian efforts to work through and support community or civil structures and thus help to reduce individual vulnerability.

8.2.3 Institutional support

Weak public capacity in many states in Africa, due to lack of investment, or government suppression of trade unions, professional associations, and national or regional civic organisations, compounds the inability of states and people to survive the destruction of war. While in politically stable environments agencies have come to see institutional development as an important empowering strategy in alleviating poverty, in situations of war such a strategy is usually eschewed in favour of commodity provision. Institutional development is replaced by neutral relief. Accountability to beneficiaries is lost in the modalities of controlling relief commodities. In the process, civic structures are further undermined, reducing the possibility of recovery.

In Somalia, the failure of the UN to re-engage early on in the conflict led to the collapse of remaining governmental structures (Slim and Visman, 1994). More thought is needed as to how organisations can work to support civic structures in the midst of war. The support for the ANC in South Africa is a recent example of this. Other examples might be the relief programmes of ERA and REST supported by NGOs during the Ethiopian conflict (Duffield and Prendergast, 1993), UNICEF's work with professional groups of teachers in Bosnia (Duffield, 1994a), Save the Children's work to rejuvenate governmental services in Somaliland, and the work of ActionAid with councils of clan elders in Somaliland (Bradbury, 1994a; IFRC, 1994). The work of groups such as the Mennonites to create 'peace constituencies' during times of conflict may also be relevant in this respect (Lederach, 1989).

ACORD's experience is that the programmes which have most successfully adapted in times of crisis and conflicts have involved investment in the development of people and organisations, and have staff have with the skills, capacities, and confidence to propose and manage activities, as well as to resolve conflicts themselves.[18] These successes have usually been premised on the previous development of a good relationship with the communities with whom they work. The presence of local staff, with their greater links into the local community and their reluctance to leave, has been crucial. Working in this way requires an ability to make political judgments and can place considerable strain on programme impartiality (see case study 5).

Case study 5: Establishing impartiality

ACORD began a programme in Huila province, Angola, in mid-1991, after the Bicesse Peace Accords had brought the fighting between the MPLA government and Unita to an end. The aim of the programme was to support the resettlement of displaced communities. A participatory methodology was used, and work began with the community of Vissapa Iela.

Despite a major division within the community, and initial distrust of ACORD, the programme team were quickly able to establish their impartiality by using participatory methods to decide upon the kinds of support needed, and who should benefit from them. The sense of community 'ownership' that resulted improved the programme's security.

An incident in 1992 illustrated the point. Unita militants entered the village with the intention of looting from, and possibly attacking, the staff. They believed ACORD was linked to the MPLA both because it worked with the government's local structures, and because ACORD's local partner, ADRA, was staffed by ex-government officials. However, the people from the community intervened to convince the militants that the programme was independent, and the militants left the village without incident. (The fact that ACORD's programme did not involve large amounts of cash or goods may also have been a contributory factor.)

As development aid declines and is replaced by relief aid, ACORD has faced problems with obtaining funding for capacity-building work. The priority of donors is to fund 'hardware' projects, such as food or infrastructural work, and they are often reluctant to support 'software' projects, such as training or institutional strengthening. Speedy delivery of equipment and medical supplies remains the hallmark of the donor and NGO response in humanitarian crises. NGOs have made major organisational investments in communications, logistics, and transport to speed up delivery systems. Less has been spent on helping people to deal with the crises themselves, or to see that delivery is effective.

Much has been written recently on institutional development and capacity building, particularly among Southern NGOs and community-based organisations (Fowler, 1992). Much of this has focused on development in a stable rather than in a turbulent environment. War creates new operating environments not only for international NGOs but also for indigenous NGOs and community-based organisations. More attention needs to be given as to how these institutions themselves manage conflict and might adapt and survive in conflict situations; and how they manage their relationship with governments and political movements.

Questions: As development aid declines can relief and development agencies continue to do development within relief budgets? How can acceptable and accountable professional, civil or religious organisations be identified to work with? How can agencies ensure their own accountability to the beneficiaries? What kinds of skills and strengths do local organisations require to sustain themselves in conflict situations?

8.2.4 Trauma

War is a deeply traumatic experience for individuals, communities, and the personnel of agency staff working in war situations. The psychological impact of conflict has been recognised for some time, for example among US Vietnam war veterans, or the victims of military repression in Latin America. In Croatia and Bosnia a large number of governmental and UN organisations and NGOs are running psychosocial programmes. In Africa less attention has been given to this aspect of conflict.

The deliberate destruction of cultural institutions and ways of life in wars may be as traumatic as individual acts of violence. In Mozambique, Liberia, Angola, and Somalia, violent acts such as the mutilation of kin by kin, and the 'cross-dressing' of warriors, suggest a total breakdown of normal societal values that cannot be explained purely by rational survival strategies. The destructive nature of war makes it relevant to ask to what extent societies can survive to provide a template for post-conflict rehabilitation. Free from societal constraints, breakdown may be so severe that social continuity and a return to normality may no longer be an option for some (Richards, 1992). The emergence of millennial cults, such as the Alice Lakwena Holy Spirit Movement (Allen, 1993) or religious fundamentalism suggests an active search for new meanings, to re-order disorder.

Provision of commodity relief is clearly an insufficient response to working in situations of conflict. Furthermore, dependency through aid, particularly among refugees, can prolong trauma and reduce the ability of people to deal with it. The failure to involve refugees, particularly women, in the administration of camps and aid programmes, or to make use of their knowledge, skills and capacities, weakens the effectiveness of the intervention and can create feelings of helplessness and exacerbate trauma (Harrell-Bond, 1986). The work of the UNHCR 'Women Victims of Violence' programme among Somali refugees in Kenya has successfully managed to involve both women and men in taking responsibility in addressing the problem of rape and trauma among women (Musse, 1993).

The applicability of Western notions of trauma as an individual condition to be treated by a trained medical professional has to be questioned in non-Western cultures. It is not clear that all societies experience trauma as an individual condition in the way in which Western medical science understands it. A community-based approach may be the most useful way of tackling the issue. However, individuals experience trauma in different ways, and some people may benefit from individual counselling, for example, after suffering sexual violence.

Most cultures have their own mechanisms ('protectors') for healing. These may include the physical reconstruction of communities, communal ceremonies, and individual treatment in the most extreme cases, such as sexual torture, where women and men may not be able to speak openly about their experiences. It is important to identify and build on these, and to adopt an integrated approach that addresses trauma as both an individual and a wider process of community reconstruction.[19] Such an approach might combine support for community reconstruction under community control, such as clearing landmines to allow rural people to resume their agriculturally-based way of life; measures to sensitise community health workers; work with local healers; or family tracing schemes. Support for the burial of the dead is one example where organisations have given attention to the problem of trauma during war.

It is essential not to relegate trauma to something that is dealt with after the conflict, but to address it as part of emergency responses during war. For example, in northern Rwanda, following the events of April 1994, ACORD encouraged the displaced in relief camps to draw on their existing skills and trades to generate incomes and supplement food distributions. By doing so it was hoped that they would regain their self-esteem and thus be better able to cope with trauma, and avoid the condition pejoratively referred to as 'dependency mentality', which results from cultural bereavement, institutionalisation within camps, and enforced inactivity.

Questions: Why have the psychological impacts of conflict only recently been recognised as an issue in Africa? Why should this issue have been given more prominence in Bosnia and Croatia, for example?

8.2.5 Human rights

The atrocities against civilians — women, children, and ethnic and religious groups — which have occurred in current conflcits have raised awareness of the need to address human rights as a development issue. The denial of human rights can generate conflict. UN peacekeeping missions have been launched and rationalised on the basis of the protection of the rights of victims. Rights are closely linked to livelihoods. For example, rights to land, rights to employment, and rights to travel affect the livelihoods of women and minority groups.

However, human rights remains a delicate issue. Human rights, self-determination, and democracy are used as rallying calls in war. Justice, freedom of religious expression, and the right to own personal property are full of cultural meaning and value. The idea of human rights being embodied in the individual, rather than as a citizen of a state, is a relatively new concept that passed into international law in the 1948 UN Universal Declaration. In Islam the *umma* (the Islamic community) is held to be more important than the State or the individual, in contrast to the rational liberalism of the West. Although humanitarian agencies advocate the protection of individual rights, actively monitoring or discussing human rights can place humanitarian agencies, and their staff, in danger, as has been the case in Rwanda.

Questions: How can organisations incorporate human rights into development and relief work? Which are the appropriate organisations to carry out this work?

8.2.6 Conflict reduction

If wars are lasting longer, one of the objectives of responding to situations of conflict should be to reduce the length of conflicts. While a de-escalation of violence may not solve the underlying causes of a conflict, it may help to prevent conflicts from becoming more protracted, mitigate vulnerability, and certainly save lives. If, as has been argued, violence disrupts people's coping strategies (section 4.3.3), then a reduction in violence can help to restore or support coping strategies. This is one argument for military interventions, peacekeeping, peace-monitoring, and safe havens.

The reduction of violence can help to create the political environment in which mediation and negotiation become feasible. Creating channels of communication can help to counter mistrust and misunderstanding and so reduce levels of violence. Active mediation and election monitoring contributed to the reduction of violence and a peaceful electoral process in South Africa. In Kenya, the UNHCR Women Victims of Violence programme is involved in educating Kenyan policemen in the rights of refugees, to reduce the incidence of violence against Somali women refugees.

During the Rwandan crisis, however, ACORD, together with several other organisations, took the view that it would not lobby for a UN-sponsored cease-fire, because the RPF's advance was the most likely force to bring an end to the massacres taking place behind the government army lines, given the absence of international action. Similarly, if the EPRDF had not defeated the Mengistu regime militarily, the war in Ethiopia would have dragged on for much longer, with greater levels of impoverishment and destruction. The Rwandan crisis has brought questions of neutrality and impartiality into sharp focus (case study 6).

Case study 6: The Rwandan crisis: impartiality, reconciliation, and justice.

The Rwandan crisis in 1994 brought into sharp focus the dilemmas surrounding questions of neutrality. At the time ACORD had two programmes in the country, and an office in Kigali. All three were devastated by the events in April, and for a number of weeks ACORD concentrated on locating staff. When an emergency programme was launched in northern Rwanda in early

May, ACORD found itself working on the RPF side of the divide between the rebels and the government.

There were a number of practical reasons for this. ACORD had experience of working in those areas, and logistical support was available from existing programmes in Uganda. With no programmes in Burundi or Zaire access to the government areas was much more difficult. Furthermore, the RPF-held zone offered a minimum guarantee of security that the government areas did not, though ACORD was determined to work in the government areas if it became possible. However, there was considerable criticism of ACORD for being supposedly pro-RPF, other agencies' interpretation of neutrality meaning that they should not work with either side, if they could only work with one.

ACORD's position was further complicated by differences in analysis with other agencies. ACORD took the view early on that there were two conflicts taking place, one a civil war between the RPF and the Rwandese army, the other an orchestrated campaign of massacres against opponents of the extremist Hutu parties. The latter presented the greatest threat to Rwandan lives, and, in light of the international community's failure to act, the RPF gave the greatest hope of ending the massacres. ACORD did not support calls for a UN-brokered ceasefire between the RPF and the army, which would have solidified the army line and allowed the massacres to continue behind it.

Once the RPF succeeded in taking control of the country, the bulk of Rwanda's population fled to refugee camps in Zaire, where they have remained, despite appalling conditions, due to fears of RPF retribution, and intimidation by the Hutu extremists, who hope to build the basis for a reinvasion of the country. Within the country the RPF has formed a new government and has appealed to the refugees to return. ACORD continues to work inside Rwanda, but has failed, due to human, financial and logistical resource constraints, to develop a programme with Rwandan refugees.

ACORD has not been neutral between the two sides to the conflict, though its position has remained impartial, and based on its mandate, and it has no political allegiance with any particular side. ACORD's fundamental aim remains to work with poor people in Rwanda, and this means the peasantry, who are mostly Hutu. However, being seen to be pro-RPF may jeopardise ACORD's ability to do this.

For the future Rwanda clearly needs a process of reconciliation. How best to go about this remains unclear. The RPF, and the UN, demand justice for the perpetrators of genocide. Yet it is clear that dividing the guilty from the innocent, when the majority took part in the massacres and have not rejected the political leadership that organised them, will be extremely difficult, if not impossible. However, without acknowledgement of, and remorse for these crimes, is reconciliation and a lasting peace possible? Should not development agencies leave to human rights bodies the responsibility for passing judgement on past atrocities, and concentrate on promoting reconciliation through community-based action?

Attempts to create 'zones of tranquillity', where fighting is controlled and violence reduced, in order to distribute relief aid have often been of limited success. It has been argued that Operation Lifeline Sudan has become integrated into sustaining the local war economy (Duffield, 1994b). In Somalia the most tranquil zones have been outside the areas where UNOSOM was keeping the peace. The economies of Croatia and Bosnia are virtually underwritten by the relief operations there, while in Bosnia, the 'peace havens' have arguably frozen the war, offering little future for those inside the havens, evidenced in the high rates of depressive illness and suicide.

Relief interventions, however, may contribute to the reduction of tension. In Somalia a blanket distribution of food by ICRC and other agencies helped to reduce looting and fighting over food supplies (IFRC, 1994). Critical to ICRC's work was the method of distribution using multiple entry-points, and ensuring the close involvement of Somalis in the distribution network. The financial cost of this operation was enormous, and the future political costs of dividing Somalia into resource distribution areas may still have to be paid.

A range of international protocols exist to protect civilians in times of war, that can contribute to the reduction of violence. Among others these include:

- The Fourth Geneva Convention (August 1949), for the protection of civilian populations in times of war;
- The UN Convention Relating to the Status of Refugees (1951), for the legal protection of refugees;
- The UN Convention on the Prevention and Punishment of the Crime of Genocide (1951), which specifically authorises the UN to take action to prevent acts of genocide;
- Weapons Convention (1980), for the restrictions on weapons that are indiscriminate;
- Landmines Protocol (1980), for regulating the use of mines.

These Conventions should in theory protect civilians in war and contribute to the reduction of violence. In all the current wars these Conventions are continually flouted. In Bosnia and Rwanda, for example, the UN failed to act to prevent genocide.

The impact of relief operations on the political and economic dynamics of wars has been noted. As their numbers grow and as their operations increase in size, NGOs are in danger of being co-opted into actions whose future consequences are unknown. In Somalia, for example, NGOs, ICRC, and the UN paid large amounts of money to free-lance militia to protect their staff, operations, and relief supplies; they thus made direct payments into the war economy. In recognition of their increased role and the impact of their operations in disaster situations, a number of NGOs have drawn up a professional Code of Conduct to set universal basic standards to govern the way in which NGOs work in providing assistance in disasters (IFRC, 1994).

Questions: What interventions can aid agencies make that can help to reduce violence? How can aid agencies monitor the impact of their own work on levels of violence? What restrictions exist that prevent the UN from acting upon the Conventions of international law?

8.2.7 Conflict resolution

What would have the greatest effect on the suffering of millions of people caught up in emergencies would be the resolution of the conflicts that have created them. While the safety-nets of humanitarian relief are an understandable and morally justifiable response to war, there is little evidence that they are addressing the root causes of armed conflict or supporting the conditions for a return to peace. If suffering, in the form of famine, refugee camps, or deepening poverty, is the result of wars, humanitarian agencies need to give some thought to what contributions they might make to resolving these conflicts.

The international community so far has failed to curb the onset of new political emergencies, or to bring an end to current conflicts. Arguably, in Somalia, Angola, Kurdistan, and Bosnia international interventions in the form of peacekeeping, peacemaking, and peace-enforcement have caused more problems than they have solved. Why have these interventions failed to stop the violence or prevent new violence from erupting? What relevance does 'conflict resolution' have to current debates? What is meant by 'sustainable' peace and can it be achieved?

A consequence of the development versus relief dichotomy is that NGOs and UN agencies have tended to take notice of conflict only after it has manifested itself in acts of violence. This is to miss the point that political violence and armed conflict are the symptoms of other problems. Long-term development which tackles issues of human rights, control over resources, power differentials, debt, and the alleviation of poverty (structural violence), might be said to be addressing the causes of conflict by transforming the conditions which generate it. However, the failure of national governments and the international community seriously to address these underlying issues means that the international community continues to be taken by surprise when conflict breaks out.

One of the weaknesses of political mediation or peacekeeping efforts in conflicts in Africa has been the concentration on 'constitutional' issues, rather than 'civil' issues (African Rights, 1993d). Conflict resolution is normally sought through constitutional negotiation and the creation of formal mechanisms for managing security, such as peacekeeping. In Sudan, Somalia, Angola, Liberia, and Bosnia, negotiations have not stopped the predatory forces which promote the wars. If anything, negotiations and the payments made to warlords to attend peace conferences, and for other services, legitimise and strengthen those forces.[20] Such negotiations detract from attempts to identify and strengthen alternative legitimate political structures.

Furthermore, negotiations by themselves are insufficient. Wars are not fought by individuals. Violence is enacted by groups of people, all of whom may have a stake in the continuation or resolution of a conflict. The resolution of a conflict requires the involvement of people at many different levels. The gunmen and fighters are as much in need of alternative means of survival as are their victims (Keen, 1994b). There is a need to understand the political and socio-economic incentives working against and for the resolution of the conflict. This may also require some reflection by NGOs on their own motives. The tendency among NGOs to assume responsibility for different geographical regions can contribute not only to the further division of those regions, but also to competition between NGOs over spheres of influence. Providing relief in war zones brings in money, pays for overheads, and is good for organisational profile. Conflict resolution may, in that sense, be less rewarding.

A framework for conflict resolution needs to distinguish between ending the violent expression of conflicts and the institutionalisation of long-term measures to prevent or mitigate conflict (Steadman, 1991). Once violence erupts, security and survival create a new set of problems that need to be addressed, one of which may be famine. At this stage there may be little to choose between neutrality or solidarity, for to some extent either stance may signify a failure not to have acted earlier.

It may be helpful to distinguish 'conflict resolution' from 'conflict management' and 'conflict settlement'. Conflict management suggests conflict is an organisational problem that can be managed by changing the conditions within institutions. Conflict settlement is concerned with negotiating 'peaceful' outcomes, which may not lead to real structural changes. Conflict resolution might be conceived of as a collaborative process of analysis and problem-solving that attempts to address the underlying issues that generate conflict (Burton, 1990).

Governments, the UN, and humanitarian agencies need to identify the level or levels at which they might support the resolution of conflicts. The armed conflicts referred to in this paper, which generate political emergencies, are large-scale regional or national wars. The NGO contribution to the settlement of these conflicts at a constitutional level is likely to be limited. The dangers of NGOs and their staff trying to mediate with warring parties and becoming co-opted or targeted by them are obvious. At the same time, NGOs working at the grassroots have a mandate and responsibility to ensure that the perceptions and needs of the weak in society are represented, and influence the policy-makers and politicians involved in political negotiations.

Furthermore, many large-scale wars have their roots in local conflicts, which may continue during the wider conflict. There may be possibilities at a local level to support civil organisations working to reduce tensions and resolve localised conflicts. Several long-established international and local NGOs, many with religious origins such as the Quakers and Mennonites, have been working on these issues for many years. There is also a growing number of secular organisations, such as International Alert. At the very least, development and relief organisations confronted with the dilemmas of new operational environments should open a dialogue with such organisations.

8.2.8 Vulnerability and conflict resolution

To date much of the emphasis of conflict prevention or resolution of internal conflicts has focused on the success and failures of international or external responses and solutions. This partly reflects the extant power relations between the conflicting parties and those who intervene. The focus has been on strengthening international or regional institutions. In the process the possibilities of internal solutions have been overlooked. Working for the reduction of violence is not the sole privilege of external agents. If conflict is inherent in human societies,

55

then mechanisms also exist within societies to manage and resolve conflicts. Mediation, peace conferences, peacekeeping, peace-enforcement, monitoring, safe-havens, humanitarian aid, and legal and judiciary procedures are just some of the overt and obvious mechanisms.

The concentration on constitutional issues means that the potential for resolution and reconciliation through civil society has been largely neglected. There is an assumption that because a society is in a state of conflict, local means of resolving conflicts no longer exist. Local peace groups, NGOs, and professional groups are currently active throughout former Yugoslavia. Evidence from Somalia and Somaliland suggests that even during the height of the war there, individuals were moving around mediating between conflicting parties in order to prevent a further escalation of war. The most sustained and successful attempts at peaceful reconciliation in Somaliland have been based on a long-term, indigenous, participatory process of conflict resolution (Yusuf, 1993; Bradbury 1994b). This has involved rebuilding the social integrity and political efficacy of Somali civil institutions, and the construction of local political alliances and agreements on the security of trade and management of resources. While the war in Somalia has clearly been more than a 'traditional' war, local solutions have been sought through adapting customary practices of conflict resolution and management. However, the legitimacy given by governments, the UN, and NGOs to these processes is minimal. Research into local processes of conflict resolution has been limited.

Involvement in conflict resolution and identifying viable structures within which to work requires a good knowledge of an area and a level of political analysis that is missing in many NGO, donor, and UN operations. However, the possible choice for organisational involvement at different levels in conflict resolution is potentially wide. In Mali ACORD was drawn into dealing with resource conflicts between pastoralists and sedentary communities. Through a process of inter-community meetings they sought to promote a negotiated solution. This involved seconding two staff members to the government to negotiate with the insurgents. This was only possible because of the long-standing relations between ACORD and the communities. Long-term working knowledge of the area also enabled ACORD to develop a range of methods for working during the 1991-92 conflict in Mali. In Ethiopia, Oxfam has supported some local negotiations over resource disputes. In Cambodia they have supported training for Buddhist monks and nuns in conflict resolution and mediation. In El Salvador they have supported training for members of the National Union of Salvadorean Workers in reconciliation and democratic processes, and given similar support to the Centre for International Studies in Nicaragua (Roseveare, 1993).

Vulnerability, and the protection of livelihoods and human rights, are the justifications for relief interventions in conflict situations. As the literature on coping strategies in famine has suggested, the means by which people attempt to make themselves less vulnerable should be a starting point for analysis and prescription in famine relief policies (Curtis et. al., 1988). Equally, the way in which people are able to continue to construct and reconstruct viable ways of life must be a starting point for analysis in situations of conflict (Allen, 1989). Understanding the conditions and processes (and perhaps costs) that make a return to peace possible might also be a starting point for relief policies in conflict situations.

Questions: What can relief and development organisations contribute to the resolution of conflicts? How can such organisations working in war identify local accountable structures, through which they can operate and which can provide a forum for reconciliation? How can these organisations work in situations of conflict in such a way that they unite rather than divide? Is it possible to restore and empower indigenous forms of peace-making and conflict resolution, and how can these contribute to overall resolution of conflicts?

8.2.9   The meaning of conflict

It has been suggested that Western concepts of conflict do not necessarily allow for 'African realities' (Bozeman, 1976). In some societies war and peace are not mutually exclusive; in 'warrior cultures', war need not be shameful, nor peace necessarily good. In the West, conflict is incompatible with civil society, while violence in the form of war is legitimate. Some of the most interesting work on conflict resolution has involved eliciting people's own understanding of conflict (HAP, 1988; Lederach, 1989). This work suggests, for example, that Western ideas of neutral mediation are incompatible with some non-Western notions of 'neutrality'. A neutral, objective approach to conflict assumes a certain neutral, objective view of the world. Clearly this has little relevance in, for example, a Muslim society (Salem, 1993). The legitimacy and authority of the mediator is not based on their distance from the fray, but their insider knowledge. Furthermore, while Western approaches to conflict resolution have tended to focus on the thoughts and impulses of individuals, other cultures recognise conflict as a group issue.

These insights are important for organisations working in situations of conflict. It has been argued that during a famine, relief activities should take a lead from local conceptions and attitudes (de Waal, 1989). Ryle's work with the Dinka in Sudan, for example, suggests that their notions of survival were different from those of relief agencies (Slim and Thompson, 1993). This was important in understanding their actions and reactions (coping strategies) during famine. Equally, the importance of listening to refugees so that they can participate in formulating plans to address their needs and fears has been stressed by a number of writers (Harrell-Bond, 1986; Wallace, 1990). In Malawi, Vaughan (1987) drew on local songs to understand how social organisation affects patterns of hunger and nutrition. In Uganda, ACORD have been using songs and proverbs to facilitate discussions between men and women about their changing roles after the conflict.

War is a social phenomenon, which uses technology. Much of relief aid in situations of conflict is still premised on a technical fix. In order to make political judgments in these situations the sociological aspects of conflict need to be better understood. The NGO Code of Conduct was drawn up with the hope of ensuring that responses to disasters are appropriate. If this Code is to be effectively implemented there is a need to find out how people think and feel about, and experience, conflict.

Question: What methods of analysis exist which can improve our understanding of different people's experiences of conflict?

8.3 Post-conflict development: the price of peace

8.3.1 The problem of peace

Although conflict resolution and peacemaking are largely alien in development literature some notion of peace has always been implicit. Development policy is often formulated in the name of stability, security, and peace. During the Cold War, poverty was perceived in the West as a threat to stability. Recently UNDP has linked development, livelihoods and security (UNDP, 1994).

Peace means different things to different people. Wars are waged in the name of peace. Pacification, a forceful form of conflict management, links peace with repression. The recent genocide in Rwanda might be seen from one perspective as an attempt to resolve a long-running conflict through a 'final solution'. It does not automatically follow that the end of violence will solve the underlying problems that generated it. The ending of the East-West nuclear confrontation has not brought an end to wars, nor done anything about changing the political structures that produced those weapons. The empowering of losers may be a solution to one conflict, but create another. Peace can have winners and losers. Attempts to impose or enforce peace by external actors is clearly fraught with problems, as seen in Somalia. Arguably, in the few cases where wars have been 'won' (e.g. in Ethiopia and Uganda) more peaceful outcomes have been achieved. However, this has also not prevented other conflicts from continuing, such as between the Oromo and the government in Ethiopia. The transition from war to peace is not easy (Case study 7).

Case study 7: Post-conflict responses

Moving to support the reconstruction of a society after a genocidal conflict like that in Rwanda clearly illustrates the potential impact that interventions can have on the likelihood of future conflicts.

Establishing the validity of competing claims to resources, and particularly land, presents a major obstacle to moving from an emergency aid to a rehabilitation programme in Rwanda. Over the last 30 years there have been successive waves of displacement out of Rwanda. Following the RPF's victory many exiles who had been living in Uganda, Tanzania, and Zaire are returning. The majority of more recent refugees remain wary of returning, intimidated by supporters of the deposed government and fearing retribution from the RPF. As a result the country is largely empty, and long-term exiles have returned to lay claim to land and property recently vacated during the current wave of displacement. ACORD must be careful not to acquire the role of arbiter in competing claims over resources, or to implicitly legitimise particular claims through its actions. To avoid this the programme intends to restrict programme support explicitly to those whose rights are generally recognised by local community structures.

However, clear problems exist. Local structures may be imbued with attitudes prejudicial to the rights of single or widowed women to own land. Following

---

the conflict it is not clear who are the authorities with legitimate powers to make these decisions. ACORD intends to consult widely with other groups, in an effort to minimise these difficulties. The new administration has a stated policy of legal resettlement for all those displaced, but whether it has the will or the resources to enforce such a policy remains unclear. However, if competing claims of a legal (recent and commonly recognised), historic (ancestral) or *de facto* nature are not resolved in a just and widely acceptable manner, disputes about resource may be the source of future conflict.

Similarly, ACORD intends to target the youth in an attempt to avert possible future conflict. Inter-generational ties have been dealt severe blows by the recent conflict. Young people, with little prospect of work or land to farm, were easily recruited into the militias, which were paid to carry out the massacres, and were largely responsible for them. If they are not to fall back on violence, banditry, and political extremism, often the result of poverty, they will need other means of supporting themselves in the future.

8.3.1 The State in post-war reconstruction

The difficulty of sustaining peace may be two-fold. Firstly, there is the question of political legitimacy of any new regime which comes to power. The battle for the hearts and minds of a population embittered by internecine war can only be won through a political consensus. This cannot rely on electoral processes or institutional democracy alone. Governments need to demonstrate their commitment to the welfare of society and to justice. A commitment to justice may include support to 'truth commissions', such as that established in El Salvador under UN auspices, or the Truth and Reconciliation Commission in South Africa. A commitment to justice also means educating people in their rights.

Secondly, the pressure on governments to provide for the needs of populations after war, and to demonstrate good governance, are enormous; but governments need resources in order to implement these commitments. A critical problem with the disengagement of the North from Africa is the lack of resources available for post-conflict development. While billions of dollars are committed to peacekeeping operations, few commitments are made for rehabilitation. In Somalia, for example, for every $10 dollars spent on military operations, only $1 was spent on rehabilitation. The outbreak of war means that embassies close and bilateral development aid is cut. As a consequence of the war in Yemen, the British government cut all bilateral aid, and the post of aid attaché at the embassy was rescinded. If Britain resumes aid, it is unlikely to be at the same level. What funds are available will be passed through NGOs.

Most of the countries afflicted by war carry heavy debt burdens. The cancellation of debts would contribute to post-war recovery and political stability. In Somalia, funds for European forces involved in Somalia were 'borrowed' from Lomé II funds allocated to Somalia, but are unlikely to be returned. To sustain the peace, people must be offered economic alternatives. This requires more development investment, not less. The role of the State and civil society is perhaps the central debate in situations of conflict. There is little evidence, however, that rational economic development as currently articulated through the nation-state model has led to peace: quite the opposite. However, whether wars can ever be settled without the over-arching authority of the State, and how that State regains legitimacy and the capacity to manage future conflicts remain fundamental questions.

If, as has been argued (section 4.1), centralised government and political control by the centre has, in part, been responsible for generating conflict, the unthinking re-establishment of structures of central state power may create the conditions for new conflicts. In post-conflict situations, the propensity of donors, the UN, and NGOs is to try to reconstruct what they recognise as government in sectors where they work. It may be better to use opportunities presented by conflicts to support the emergence of local, rather than centralised, political structures, that will ensure autonomy and local management (Shepherd, 1992). Supporting the devolution of power does not reduce the need to ensure the support and participation of marginal groups in any new local political structures.

Where the State and its institutions have been destroyed, undermined, or radically altered through conflict, agencies must consider how best to position themselves with the State-civil society duality. It is not the role of NGOs to substitute for the State, yet they may find it impossible to function without doing so, or at least propping up inappropriate state machinery. In Niassa province, Mozambique, for example, ACORD has been providing support to the provincial government since 1989, in order to strengthen the capacity of local government to promote decentralised development activities. In retrospect, it might have been better advised to focus more directly on supporting grassroots structures.

Since the 'Age of Enlightenment', peace in the West has been linked to material and moral progress. It is wrong to place conflict and peace at different ends of the spectrum of development. It might be better to de-link the notion of peace and development conceived as progress, or at least to accept that there may be alternative forms of development.

8.3.2 Demobilisation

Large-scale demobilisation poses a major problem in most conflict-affected areas. Demobilised fighters face specific problems of reintegration. They have often been brutalised by their experiences and find it difficult to fit back into their old social roles; and they may be injured or disabled. Furthermore, they are returning to economies often bankrupted by war and in which everyone is struggling to survive. The skills they have learnt as soldiers may be of little use in making a living other than through banditry. In Mali the recent outbreak of violence is linked to the inability of demobilised Tamasheq fighters to find employment either in the regular army or in the civilian economy.

In El Salvador, Mozambique, and Malawi, Oxfam have provided support for demobilisation programmes (Roseveare, 1993). In Somaliland, UNDP-OPS commissioned Zimbabweans with experience of demobilisation in Zimbabwe to advise the new administration on demobilisation there. Lack of funding, however, severely hampered that programme. In Eritrea, ACORD has plans to train ex-fighters as 'barefoot bankers' for a credit scheme, and train groups of ex-fighters as economic units (e.g. in brick and tile making) in order to use their experience of team-work. However, such schemes can only reach a few people. Furthermore, demobilisation programmes which focus on providing finance, training, and support to ex-fighters often fail to address the psychological and social problems they and their families face on their return to civilian life. Finding a new economic role for tens of thousands of ex-combatants is a major challenge for governments and administrations in post-conflict situations. It is clearly not something that NGOs alone can tackle.

Questions: How can governments, the UN, NGOs, and others support demobilisation of combatants? Where has demobilisation been successfully carried out and what lessons can be drawn from these examples?

8.4 Operational issues

Crisis situations often magnify weak points in organisational management, yet an effective response in situations of armed conflict depends on organisational capacity. Successful adaptation to working in situations of conflict will require defining in advance organisational procedures and guidelines for working should conflict erupt (case study 8). The following section looks at some operational issues which organisations need to address in working in conflict situations.

Case study 8: The need for preparedness

ACORD's programme in Sablaale, Somalia, has been severely destabilised by the conflict in the country. Targeting of programme activities became extremely difficult as a constantly changing population in Sablaale made previously gathered baseline data unreliable. ACORD was forced to respond to the changes, most notably in the number of female-headed households, on a day-to-day basis while trying to provide food relief. Unfortunately, because of a loss of senior staff in the area, ACORD did not have in place sufficient expertise to do this. This contributed to the local elders' ability to control and manipulate the distribution of food.

It may be the case that no one, no matter what their background, could have coped in such a situation. However, the development of specific systems and operational guidelines for conflict, or the direct involvement of local community groups counter-balancing the influence of the elders, as has been done more recently, might well have facilitated a more effective response.

8.4.1 Staffing and management

In conflicts field teams are often cut off from their headquarters at the time that they are most in need of support (case study 9). Senior staff may be absent for periods of time, while others might be killed or displaced. National staff come under considerable stress during conflicts. They may be forced into taking sides or suffer personal trauma. If field staff are inadequately supported they will have difficulty in responding with flexibility to emergencies. Meeting the needs of staff is therefore an important aspect of organisational management in conflict situations.

Case study 9: Operational problems in conflict

ACORD's programme in Juba has experienced considerable operational problems. For sustained periods the town was only accessible by air. The expatriate Programme Coordinator (PC) was often absent due to the insecurity, while a number of senior staff members were displaced by a major SPLA offensive in 1992. Communications were cut off, the programme's radio was confiscated, and for a number of years the programme has relied on the World Food Programme mail-pouch and radio. Representatives from the Secretariat and the Regional Support Structure (RSS) were unable to visit the programme for considerable periods.

As a result the programme became increasingly isolated, both physically and psychologically. Monitoring and evaluation, and reporting fell upon relatively junior members of staff, who were insufficiently trained and experienced for these roles. Programme quality inevitably suffered.

The experience in Juba illustrates the need for greater efforts to provide for communications and information flows during conflicts. However, it is inevitable that communications will suffer, and consequently, teams must be equipped with the ability to maintain programme quality should they become isolated.

The quality of programming in conflict situations clearly depends to a large extent on the capacities of the staff, and the quality of support they receive from headquarters. In emergency situations there is a tendency among NGOs to revert to relying on international staff. A problem that faces UN, NGOs, and donor agencies which rely on expatriate personnel is the high turn-over of staff and the lack of institutional memory. Considerable effort therefore needs to be invested in strengthening the capacities of local staff and equipping them with the skills, tools, and confidence to cope in such situations that will diminish the need for distance management.

ACORD's recent experience in Somalia illustrates the extreme difficulties of long-distance management in such conditions. Staff on the ground were unprepared to cope, and unsupported, in a situation of extreme unrest. Attempts to control operations from Nairobi and London failed because no effective communications strategy under conflict conditions had been agreed upon beforehand. Guidelines concerning communication and reporting clearly need to be in place before a conflict begins; once it starts it is too late. Furthermore, a strong managing presence is also required on the ground, with at least occasional access to the programme area.

Preparedness can involve a variety of measures including a review of the most appropriate organisational structures for working in conflict situations. Team-based structures, rather than hierarchical structures, may be more capable of responding with the flexibility required. Reducing the operational presence of international NGOs, and supporting local NGOs or community organisations, may be an even better. strategy

In its programmes in the Horn of Africa, ACORD is currently attempting to incorporate these lessons into its programming. So far efforts have focused on the development of a series of indicators and a monitoring system to detect signs of turbulence, improve a programme's preparedness for it, and aid decision-making should conflict affect the programme. The indicators (on the level of communications, reporting, financial controls, managerial control, programme activities, relations with the communities, team composition, and security) are to be monitored on a regular basis, as part of normal monthly reporting requirements.

This is very much 'work in progress', an attempt to develop simple tools for monitoring programmes and their preparedness, using key indicators. The expectation is that these tools will be tested during programme activities, and that changes will be made accordingly. They are meant to aid, and not substitute for, the management process, principally by providing a mechanism which regularly raises relevant issues. Any final decision will require judgements, not only on these issues but also on likely future prospects.

ACORD have concluded that team cohesion, and team-building skills within programmes are the most important factors in enabling programmes to work in conflict situations. Programmes with a strong team ethic cope well with absences of staff members. This approach involves ensuring a balance between multi-skilled staff and specialists. The composition of teams along gender and ethnic lines can be crucial to team cohesion, and perceptions of an agency's impartiality. Achieving a programme of well-trained and supported 'frontline staff', who are able to maintain programme quality, while isolated for periods of time, requires investment in people prior to conflicts. For ACORD, this has been something difficult to fund.

8.4.2 Communications

Communications are vital in conflict situations not only to maintain information flows, but also to provide psychological and other support to programme teams. If information flows and reporting were problematic in normal conditions, they are likely to worsen in situations of conflict. Communications systems such as radios are often an early target of military forces. Often, it is the technology of agencies that make them a specific target for armies and banditry. To overcome this agencies have increasingly invested in security by hiring armed guards, with implications for impartiality and their contributions to the war. Finding a way to maintain effective information flows and preparing these in advance, will go some way to ensuring an ability to support staff and continue to manage programmes.

ACORD's experience has been that some programmes are able to carry out very good work when communications have been impossible, due to good relationships with the communities and cohesive, capable teams. Strengthening people's abilities to cope and respond flexibly to conflict situations is as important as the technology of communication, and should go hand in hand with the efforts to maintain communication systems.

8.4.3 Responsibilities

When a conflict breaks out in a country where an agency is working questions arises about staying or leaving. While staying on has often been valuable in linking emergency work to longer-term development there may be costs attached in terms of risks to staff and resources. Clarity in each situation of the costs and benefits of staying on is difficult to obtain. Some agencies (such as ICRC or MSF) have clear mandates and structures, which enable them to take certain risks. A key indicator for many agencies is whether agency staff are being deliberately targeted.

> **Case study 11: Programme suspensions**
>
> ACORD's programme in Gulu district, northern Uganda was repeatedly suspended between 1985 and 1988, due to conflict. At the time the programme was managed by expatriates who were based in Kampala. Within the Gulu team there remains considerable resentment about the unparticipatory and abrupt manner in which decisions to suspend programmes were made and communicated to programme staff. This resentment is heightened by the continuation of programming activities between 1991 and 1992, when the conflict was more violent. With the increasing willingness of NGOs to work in conflict situations, and the nationalisation of ACORD teams, these problems are likely to recur. In the future it will be important to maintain open and transparent dialogue about these issues, and establish guidelines about how staff are treated.

Most agencies are increasingly confronted with these issues in the course of their work. In Rwanda, events happened so quickly that there was no time for questions of programme suspension, Instead, ACORD made considerable efforts to trace staff and to rescue others whose lives were under threat.[21] These efforts were not helped by the UN's restriction of airlifts to expatriate staff. Arrangements were made to pay those that were found alive, and to include them in future programmes, if they so wished. However, there were considerable problems with redeployment to other programmes due to security problems elsewhere.

In the event of programme suspension or closure, the responsibilities agencies have for their local staff and dependents is often unclear and poorly handled. The UN's restriction of air evacuation procedures to expatriate staff provided a stark reminder of the need to address these issues so that all staff are afforded the same protection and support in conflict situations. While terms and conditions among agencies differ, a pooling of experiences on such issues might prove extremely valuable.

Questions: What forms of organisational structure are best suited for aid agencies working in conflict situations? What training and skills can best prepare staff for working in these situations? What responsibilities do organisations have for their employees working in situations of conflict?

8.5 Advocacy and policy reform

Although agencies claim to design their interventions on the basis of need, in practice various factors determine how choices are made and which needs are responded to. The humanitarian assistance policies of major donors and the UN are among those factors delineating the political and financial criteria within which agencies such as NGOs can operate. For example, the lack of official recognition for the Somaliland government has inhibited several agencies from working in that country. If official aid to a country is suspended, for human rights reasons, long-term development programmes may suffer financial cut-backs, thus compounding the injustices being meted out to the population. The distinction between 'development' and 'humanitarian' work often has more to do with the political positions taken by governments than the demands and potential of the situation on the ground.

Increasingly, the direct involvement of governments, the UN, and their military in humanitarian activities, is having a marked effect on the political and military profile of the wars themselves, as seen clearly in Bosnia, Somalia and Rwanda (section 7.1). High-profile and high-spending involvement creates its own dynamic in terms of population movements, markets and employment, prices, and the expectations of the population. At the same time, the UN is constrained by lack of resources from operating effectively and meeting its stated commitments. For example, in Bosnia donor commitments of peacekeeping forces have fallen way behind requests. In Rwanda, the US and British governments were unable to provide transport for African peacekeeping forces when requested. And yet within hours of Iraq threatening a second invasion of Kuwait, the US and British governments were able to send thousands of troops.

The inconsistency of international responses to these conflicts makes it imperative that NGOs working in conflict-prone areas develop mechanisms to influence the policy environment in which their operational and financial plans evolve. This includes, *inter alia*, influencing the media which themselves create pressures on governments; encouraging official preventive diplomacy and conflict resolution; pressing for UN reforms; and attempting to secure agreements on limiting the scope of the arms trade.

Questions: What are the key policy issues that relief and development organisations, donors, the UN, and other NGOs, should be working on in the light of current conflicts?

8.6 Thinking about conflict

For a number of humanitarian agencies formed in response to situations of war, armed conflict and civil disturbance has always been a strategic issue in the relief of poverty. For others this is new and uncertain territory. This paper has suggested some issues that agencies may need to address in responding to situations of armed conflict.

What are the best ways of instituting change within an organisation to take account of these issues? Should donor agencies, for example, adapt by becoming operational? Should agencies adopt human rights into their mission statements? Should agencies train staff in conflict resolution? Rather than 'skilling up' the organisation, would an alternative be to strengthen other organisations and individuals? What is the process that agencies can go through in thinking through these options?

Oxfam in 1990, ACORD in 1993, and ActionAid in 1994, have all held workshops in Uganda to discuss the implications of conflict for their organisations. Oxfam commissioned a number of studies to complement this, including a review of Oxfam's work in conflict situations (Agerbak, 1991), on the relationship between war and famine in Africa (Duffield, 1990), the psychological impact of war (Summerfield, 1990), the sources of training in mediation (Fisher, 1990). In 1992 Save the Children convened a meeting on conflict and relief in African famines (Petty et. al. 1992). ActionAid are in the process of commissioning a study on conflict resolution and have established an internal learning group on peace, conflict, and reconciliation. As part of work on conflict issues, ACORD has convened a network on conflict, development, and peace (CODEP), which brings together NGOs, donors, and academics. In 1994, the European Liaison Committee to the European Community convened a conference on 'Conflict, Development and Military Intervention'. In 1994, IDS and IIED convened a workshop on conflict resolution and PRA. A number of agencies have sent staff for training with the Responding to Conflict Programme.

Information networks have been established in response to some specific conflicts. These include the British Agencies Afghanistan Group, and the Gulf Information Network based at the British Refugee Council, and the Inter-NGO Committee for Somalia. Is there a need for another agency that can monitor and gather information, rather than establishing *ad hoc* committees?

Crises produce quick reactions, but crises also demand thought. Engineers, medical teams, logisticians, and administrators, rarely have the time to think beyond the nuts and bolts of delivering aid. To understand the causes and consequences of conflict and the impact of relief interventions there is a need for a variety of social, economic, and political analysis. This means that organisations may need to become more intellectually resourced. There is a need to move beyond the constraints of 'logical frameworks' and to consider what forms of analysis can best serve organisations in identifying the strategic issues in conflict situations. With a rapid turnover of staff in emergencies, institutional memory is quickly lost; how can this knowledge be retained?

Questions: To what extent have these initiatives changed the way that aid organisations are thinking about and working in conflict situations? How can organisations think about conflict, and turn thoughts into policy and policy into action? What resources are available to help them do this?

NOTES

1 The full case studies are available on request from ACORD.

2 The fall of the Berlin Wall was preceded by a number of significant nuclear arms treaties in the 1980s, such as the 1987 Intermediate-Range Nuclear Forces Treaty, which also contributed to the reduction of this fear.

3 The number of wars taking place at any one time, and the exact numbers of war casualties, depend upon how a 'war' is defined. According to the Stockholm International Peace Research Institute (SIPRI, 1987-1992) there have been 165 major armed conflicts since 1945 (35 in Africa), which have resulted in 40 million deaths. If the definition of armed conflict is extended to include genocides, democides, and ethnocides, 160 million people have been killed by their governments this century (Rupesinghe, 1992). A generally accepted definition of a major armed conflict is one involving more than 1,000 battle-field deaths. Despite agreement on this criterion there are inconsistencies in the records. Few official records are kept, especially of civilian deaths. SIPRI's emphasis on accumulated battle deaths means that civilian massacres and genocides are not taken into account.

4 The term 'low-intensity warfare' was applied to a number of conflicts during the 1980s, particularly in Latin America, to describe wars of destabilisation by powerful states against others using proxy guerrilla forces (for example in Nicaragua and Mozambique). While the wars may have been low-intensity from the point of view of the aggressors, the effects were far different for the victims.

5 Language is rarely neutral. These labels reflect a change in the meaning of war and in the perception of power relations. The labels 'local', 'low intensity', 'regional', or 'domestic' (applied by the North) describe wars taking place 'elsewhere'; and perhaps help to distance the North from any responsibility for them (Miller, 1992). For the purpose of this paper the term 'internal war' will be used as it reflects a theme of the paper: that responses to these wars require an understanding of the historical particularity of the context in which the wars are taking place.

6 The end of the Cold War, the economic strength of East Asian countries, and the economic crisis in Eastern Europe and the former Soviet Union have created a problem with terminology used to describe what was already a heterogeneous range of countries. The term 'Third World' might now be more applicable to the former Soviet Union, than countries in East Asia (Berger, 1994). For the purpose of this paper the term 'South' is mainly used.

7 This concern is reflected in a growing literature among British NGOs since 1990 on the implications of the rise of armed conflict in the South: Agerbak 1991, Duffield, 1990; Panos, 1991; ACORD, 1991; ActionAid, 1993; Save the Children Fund, 1991.

8 The model of modern nation states can be traced to the 1648 Treaty of Westphalia.

9 This in part is due to the way in which 'security' expenditure is hidden. In South Africa, for example, the secret service was funded by the Finance Ministry, and 'homeland' armies from the development budget. Actual expenditure was usually higher than requested (Ball, 1991; 277-278).

10 These commercial links are one explanation for the refusal of the Nigerian military to hand over power to a civilian government. Commentators have noted similar links between the new military government in the Gambia and the military in Sierra Leone, Nigeria, and Ghana, all members of the ECOMOG 'peacekeeping' force in Liberia (Dowden, Independent, 12/8/94).

11 This section draws on the work of Duffield on war and famine in Africa (1990) and subsequent work on 'complex emergencies' (Duffield 1992; 1993 with Prendergast; 1994a; 1994b; 1994c), and the parallel work of writers such as de Waal (1989; 1990; 1993) and Keen (1992).

12 This is reflected in the decline in, for example, British diplomatic representation in African countries. The British Foreign Office has stated, for example, that it would never reopen an embassy in Somalia. In many instances, NGOs now provide an essential channel of information for foreign ministries.

13 This form of war economy can also seen Bosnia, where 'warlords' have profited from the war. The Bosnian Serb leader Karadzic, for example, has been accused of profiteering (Independent 7/8/94). Significantly, UN peacekeeping contingents have also been accused of war profiteering (Ashdown, 'Bosnia: No way to run a war', Independent 8/8/94).

14 Relief for Rwandan refugees in Zaire, who include members of the former government and army who carried out genocide, might be an extreme example.

15 This draws on the work of ACORD, 1992b.

16 This section draws on the work of el Bushra and Piza-Lopez, 1994a.

17 The financial costs of peacekeeping are placing enormous economic strain on the UN. As of May 1993 contributions by Member States amounted to only $1.4 billion. The UN's problems stem partly from the financial squeeze placed on the UN by the Reagan administration in the 1980s, which perceived the UN as politically biased and financially irresponsible.

18 ACORD, December 1991. Also ACORD's case studies of programmes in Mali, Sudan, Uganda, and Angola.

19 See Summerfield, D (1994) 'Reflections on refugees and violence' in *Refugee Participation Network* 16. Also 'Charting human responses to extreme violence and the limitations of Western psychiatric models: an overview', paper presented to the World Conference on Trauma and Tragedy, Amsterdam, June 1992; and (n.d.) 'The impact of war and atrocity on civilian populations: an overview of major themes', mimeo; Gibbs, S (1994) 'Post-war social reconstruction in Mozambique: re-framing children's experience of trauma and healing' in *Disasters* 18(3):268-76.

20 It was reported that, at the time that UNOSOM II was offering a reward for General Aideed, he was also receiving regular payments from the UN for his forces, for facilitating the peaceful landing of US Marines from UNITAF. Also see Vines, 1994 on Renamo.

21 In spite of these efforts 12 staff members of ACORD lost their lives in the Rwandan crisis.

BIBLIOGRAPHY

ACORD (1991a) *Famine and Conflict in Africa: Challenges for Acord,* London: ACORD.

ACORD (1991b) *Operationality in Turbulence: the Need for Change,* London: ACORD.

ACTIONAID, ICVA, EUROSTEP (1994) *The Reality of Aid,* London.

African Rights (1993a March) *The Marginalized Peoples of Northern Sudan.* London.

African Rights (1993b May) *Somalia, Operation Restore Hope: A Preliminary Assessment.* London.

African Rights (1993c July) *Somalia: Human Rights Abuses by the United Nations.* London.

African Rights (1993d December) *Components of A Lasting Peace in Sudan: First Thoughts, Discussion Paper No.2.* London.

African Rights (1994 May) *Rwanda: Who is Killing; Who is Dying; What is Being Done.* London.

Agerbak L. (1991) 'Breaking the cycle of violence: doing development in situations of conflict, *Development in Practice,* 1 (3): pp 151-8. Oxfam.

Allen, T. (1989) 'Violence and Moral Knowledge: Observing Social Trauma in Sudan and Uganda.' in *Cambridge Anthropology: Special Issue on Local Warfare in Africa* Department of Social Anthropology, Cambridge, Vol 13, no 2, 1988-89: pp 45-65.

Allen, T. (1993) 'Understanding Alice: Uganda's Holy Spirit Movement in context', *Africa,* Vol 61, No 3.

Ashdown, P. (1994) 'Bosnia: No way to run a war', *Indepndent,* 8/8/94.

Ball, N. (1991) 'The effect of conflict on the economies of Third World countries.' in Deng and Zartman (eds), *Conflict Resolution in Africa,* Brookings Institute, Washington: pp 272-292.

Bastian, S. (1993) *Towards and Intervention Strategy in a Conflict Situation: A Case Study of Amparai and Batticaloa,* Sri Lanka, ITDG.

Berger, T.M., (1994) 'The end of the Third World?' in *Third World Quarterly,* Vol 15, No 2. pp 256-272.

Borton, J., (1993) 'Recent trends in the international relief system', *Disasters* Vol 17.3, September.

Boutros-Ghali, B. (1992) *An Agenda for Peace.* New York. United Nations.

Bozeman, A.B. (1976) *Conflict in Africa: Concepts and Realities,* Princeton University Press.

Bradbury, M. (1994a), 'The case of the yellow setee: experiences of doing development in post-war Somaliland', *Community Development Journal,* Vol 29, No 2: pp 113-122.

Bradbury, M. (1994b) *The Somali Conflict: Prospects for Peace,* Oxfam Research Paper no 9.

Burton, J. (1990) *Conflict: Resolution and Provention.* London: Macmillan.

Chambers, R. (1983) *Rural Development: Putting the Last First.* England: Longman.

Chambers, R. (1993) *Challenging the Professions.* London: IT.

Clark, J. (1991) *Democratizing Development: The Role of Voluntary Organizations,* London: Earthscan Publications.

Curtis, D., Hubbard, M., Shepherd, A., (1988) *Preventing Famine: Policies and Prospects for Africa*. London: Routledge.

Deng, F.M., Zartman, I.W., (1991) *Conflict Resolution in Africa*. Washington: Brookings Institute.

de Waal, A., (1990) 'A reassessment of entitlement theory in the light of recent famines', in *Development and Change*, Vol 21, pp 469-490.

de Waal, A., (1989) *Famine that Kills: Darfur, Sudan, 1984-1985*. Oxford: Clarendon Press.

Dreze, E. and Sen, A., (1989) *Hunger and Public Action*. Oxford: OUP.

Drysdale, J. (1994) *Whatever Happened to Somalia?* London: HAAN.

Duffield, M. (1990) *War and Famine in Africa*. Oxford: Oxfam.

Duffield, M. and Prendergast, J, (1993) *Neutrality and Humanitarian Assistance: The Emergency Relief Desk and The Cross-Border Operation Into Eritrea and Tigray*, Birminham University, UK and Centre of Concern, Washington.

Duffield, M. (1994a) *Complex Political Emergencies: An Exploratory Report for UNICEF with Reference to Angola and Bosnia*, Birmingham School of Public Policy.

Duffield, M., (1994b) 'The political economy of internal war: asset transfer and the internationalisation of public welfare in the Horn of Africa', in Macrae, J. (ed) *Wars of Hunger*. London: Zed Press.

Duffield, M.,(1994c) Complex emergencies and the crisis of developmentalism, *IDS Bulletin: Linking Relief and Development*, Vol 25, No 3 October 1994. W:G7

Dutch Government (1993) *Humanitarian Aid: Between Conflict and Development*, Ministry of Foreign Affairs, The Hague.

El Bushra, J. and Piza Lopez, E., (1994a) *Development in Conflict: The Gender Dimension, Report on the Oxfam AGRA East Workshop on Conflict and Gender, Pattaya, Thailand, 1-4 February 1993*. Oxfam UK/I and ACORD.

El Bushra, J., and Piza-Lopez, E., (1994b) 'Gender, war and food' in Macrae, J. (ed) *Wars of Hunger*. London: Zed Press.

EPAG (July 1994) *An Investigation into Trade and Commerce in the Southern Sudan, Part 1: A Report on the Informal Trade Networks Operating Between Western Upper Nile, Jonglei, Upper Nile and Northern Sudan*. Nairobi.

Finucane, A., (1993) 'The changing roles of voluntary organizations', in Cahill, K.M. (ed) *A Framework for Survival: Health, Human Rights and Humanitarian Assistance in Conflicts and Disasters*. New York: Basic Books and the Council on Foreign Relations.

Fisher, S. (1990) *Mediation and Training Agencies*. Oxford: Oxfam.

Fowler, A. (1992) *Institutional Development and NGOs in Africa*. UK: Intrac/Novib.

Fukui, K., (1994) 'Conflict and ethnic interaction: the Mela and their neighbours.' in K. Fukui and J. Markakis (ed) *Ethnicity and Conflict in the Horn of Africa*. London: James Currey Ltd: pp 33- 47.

Galtung J. (1990) 'Violence and peace.' in Smoker Davies and Munske (ed) *A Reader in Peace Studies*, Pergamon: pp 9-14.

Gantzel, K.J. (1994) 'War in the Post-World-War-II-World: Empirical Trends, Theoretical Approaches and Problems in the Concept of Ethnic War'. Paper presented at the Symposium on Ethnicity and War, San Marino: Centre for InterdisciplinaryResearch on Social Stress.

Gibbs, S. (1994) 'Post-war social reconstruction in Mozambique: re-framing children's experience of trauma and healing, in *Disasters* Vol.18, no. 3, pp 268-276.

Gueye, M.B. (1994) 'Conflicts and alliances between farmers and herders: a case study of the 'Goll' of Fandene village, Senegal', *IIED Dryland Network Programme, Issue Paper* no 49, April. London.

Harrell-Bond (1986) *Imposing Aid: Emergency Assistance to Refugees*, Oxford: OUP.

Harrell-Bond (1993) *Creating Marginalised Dependent Minorities: Relief Programmes for Refugees in Europe*. RSP 15, September 1993.

(HAP) Horn of Africa Project (1989) *Facing the Enemy: Conflict Resolution Rooted in the Horn of Africa*. Ontario, Canada.

Howell, S., and Willis, R., (1989) *Societies at Peace: Anthropological Perspectives*. London: Routledge.

Human Rights Watch (1993) *The Lost Agenda: Human Rights and UN Field Operations*. USA

International Federation of the Red Cross Societies (IFRC) (1994), *World Disasters Report*, Netherlands.

Karam, K.M. (1980) 'Dispute Settlement Among Pastoral Nomads in the Sudan', MSc Development Administration. Birmingham University.

Keen, D. (1992) *A Political Economy of Refugee Flows From South-West Sudan, 1986-1988*, UNRISD.

Keen, D. (1994a) *The Benefits of Famine: A Political Economy of Famine and Relief in Southwestern Sudan, 1983-1989*. Princeton, NJ: Princeton University Press.

Keen, D. (1994b) 'Feeding Off Disaster: It's time to address the functions of famine and "anarchy"'. Unpublished.

Kitching, G. (1990) *Development and Underdevelopment in Historical Perspective*. London: Routledge.

Korten, D. C. (1990) *Setting to the 21st Century: Voluntary Action and the Global Agenda*. Connecticut: Kumarian Press.

Lamphear, J. (1994) 'The evolution of Ateker "New Model Armies": Jie and Turkana', in K. Fukui and J. Markarkis (eds), *Ethnicity and Conflict in the Horn of Africa*, Eastern Africa Studies. London: Jamed Currey. pp 217-239.

Lane, C., and Swift, J. (1989) East African Pastoralism: Common Land, Common Problems: Report on the Pastoral Land Tenure Workshop, Arusha, Tanzania 1988, *IDS Issue Paper* No.8. June.

Lederach, J.P. (1989) 'Conflict transformation: the case for peace advocacy' in Wiebe, M. (ed) *NGOs and Peacemaking: A Prospect for the Horn*. Horn of Africa Project. Institute of Peace and Conflict Studies, Conrad Grebel College, Ontario, Canada.

Lewis, I.M. (1988) *A Modern History of Somalia*. Colorado: Westview Press.

Lewis, I.M. (1993) 'Misunderstanding the Somali crisis', *Anthropology Today*, Vol. 9, No. 4. August. pp 1-2.

Macrae, J. and Zwi, A. (1992) *Conflict and International Relief in Contemporary African Famines, Report of a Meeting Convened by SCF and the Health Policy Unit, London School of Hygiene and Tropical Medicine*, Petty, White, Macrae, Zwi (eds).

Macrae, J., Zwi, A., Birungi, H. (1993) *A Healthy Peace?: Rehabilitation nd Development of the Health Sector in a Post-Conflict Situation — The Case of Uganda*, London School of Hygiene and Tropical Medicine.

Markakis, J., (ed) (1993) *Conflict and the Decline of Pastoralism in the Horn of Africa*, Institute of Social Studies and Macmillan Press, London.

Markakis, J (1994) 'Ethnic conflict and the State in the Horn of Africa'. in Fukui, K. and Markakis, J. (eds) *Ethnicity and Conflict in the Horn of Africa*. Eastern Africa Studies. London: James Currey. pp 217-239.

Mauss, M., (1974) *The Gift*. London: Routledge and Kegan Paul.

Miller, N, N. (1981) 'The Other Somalia: Part 1 — Illicit Trade and the Hidden Economy.' *American Universities Field Staff Reports* (Queen Elizabeth House Oxford) (29): p 1-17

Miller, R., (1992) *Aid as Peacemaker: Canadian Development Assistance and Third World Conflict* Ottowa: Carleton University Press.

Mitchell, C.R., and Webb, K. (1988) *New Approaches to International Mediation*,

Musse, F. (1993) *Refugee Women Victims of Violence*, UNHCR.

NCO (National Committee for Development Education) (February 1994) *Report of Conference on Development and Conflict*, Holland.

Nordstrom, C. (1992) 'The dirty war: civilian experience of conflict in Mozambique and Sri Lanka.' in Rupesinghe (ed), *Internal Conflict and Governance* UK: St Martin's Press, Macmillan Press. pp 27-44.

Norgaard, R. B. (1994) *Development Betrayed: The End of Progress and a Coevolutionary Revisioning of the Future*. London: Routledge.

Odhiambo, A. (1991) 'The Economics of Conflict Among Marginalised Peoples of Eastern Africa.' in Deng and Zartman (eds), *Conflict Resolution in Africa* Washington: Brookings Institute.

Perez, A. (1992) 'The International Centre for Human Rights and Democratic Development: a new approach to politics and democracy in developing countries?' in Miller, R. (ed) *Aid as Peacemaker: Canadian Development Assistance and Third World Conflict* Ottowa: Carleton University Press.

Pilger, J. (1993) *The US Fraud in Africa*, New Statesman and Society.

Porter, D. et al, (1991) *Development in Practice: Paved with Good Intentions*. London: Routledge.

Prior, J. (1994) *Pastoral Development Planning*, Oxfam Development Guidelines 9. Oxford, Oxfam.

Petty, C., Macrae, J., White, J., Zwi, A. (1992) *Conflict and International Relief in Contemporary African Famines*, report of a meeting convened by SCF-UK and Health Policy Unit, LSHTM.

Redclift, M. (1984) *Development and the Environmental Crisis*, Routledge, London, 1984.

Richards, P. (1992) 'Famine (and war) in Africa', in *Anthropology Today*, Vol. 8, No. 6. pp3-5.

Rondinelli, D.A. (1993) *Development Projects as Policy Experiments*, Routledge, London.

Roseveare, N. (1993) 'Demobilization: Post-Conflict Issues and Work, An Oxfam Review' (unpublished).

Rupesinghe, K. (1989) *Conflict Resolution in Uganda*. Oslo:International Peace Research Institute (IPRI).

Rupesinghe, K. (1992a) 'The Role of Non-Governmental Organisations in Early Warning and Conflict Resolution', unpublished paper.

Rupesinghe, K. (1992b) *Internal Conflict and Governance*. New York: St Martins Press.

Sachs, W. (1993) *The Development Dictionary*. London: Zed Books.

Salem, P. E. (1993) 'Cross-Cultural Perspectives: Thoughts on Western Conflict Resolution in an Arab Context', draft paper presented to the AUB Conference on Conflict Resolution, Larnaca, Cyprus, July 1993.

Samatar, Ahmed, I. (ed) (1994) *The Somali Challenge: From Catastrophe to Renewal?*, Lynne Rienner, Boulder, London.

Schrijvers, J., (1993) *The Violence of Development: A Choice for Intellectuals.* Netherlands: INDRA.

Sen, A., (1986) *Poverty and Famines.* Oxford: Clarendon.

Shepherd, A. (1992) *Dream of Development: Somalia UNDP Project Plan, 1983-1986.*

Shepherd, A. (forthcoming) *Sustainable Rural Development.*

Shiva, V., (1991) *The Violence of the Green Revolution: Third World Agriculture, Ecology and Politics* London: Zed Books.

Slim, H. and Mitchell, J. 'Towards community-managed relief: a case study from Southern Sudan', in *Disasters* Vol 14, No 4: pp 265-269.

Slim, H. and Thompson, P. (1993) *Listening for a Change: Oral Testimony and Development*, London: Panos Publications.

Slim, H. and Visman, E., (1994) *Evacuation, Intervention and Retaliation: United Nations Humanitarian Operations in Somalia 1991-1993*, SCF/Pinter forthcoming.

Smith, A.D. (1986) 'Conflict and collective identity: class ethnie and nation'. in Burton and Azar (ed), *International Conflict Resolution: Theory and Practice*, Wheatsheaf Books: pp 63 — 83

Summerfield, D.A. (1990) 'The Psychological Effects of Conflict in the Third World: A Short Study', unpublished paper for Oxfam.

Summerfield, D.A. (1994) 'Reflections on refugees and violence' in *Refugees Participation Network*, 16.

Suhrke, A. (1993), March. 'A crisis diminished: refugees in the developing world'. *International Journal* XLVIII: pp 215-239.

Turton, D., (1989) 'Warfare, vulnerability and survival: a case from South-western Ethiopia.' in *Cambridge Anthropology: Special Issue on Local Warfare in Africa* Department of Social Anthropology, Cambridge, Vol 13, no 2, 1988-89: pp 67-85.

Turton, D. (1994) 'Mursi political identity and warfare: the survival of an idea.' in Fukui and Markakis (eds), *Ethnicity and Conflict in the Horn of Africa*. London: James Currey Ltd: p 15- 31.

Twose, N. (ed) (1991) *Greenwar* London: Panos.

United Nations (1986) *Everyone's United Nations: A Handbook on the Work of the United Nations*, UN, New York. United Nations.

United Nations (1993) *United Nations Peace-keeping*. New York: United Nations.

United Nations (1994) October 18. *Report of the Secretary-General: Strengthening of the Coordination of Humanitarian Emergency Assistance of the United Nations A/48/536*. New York: United Nations.

UNDP (1992) *Human Development Report*. New York.

UNDP (1994) *Human Development Report*. New York.

(USCR) US Committee for Refugees) (1993) *World Refugee Survey*, Washinhington.

Vaughan, M. (1987) *The Story of an African Famine: Gender and Famine in Twentieth Century Malawi*, Cambridge University Press.

Vines, A. (1994) *No Democracy Without Money: The Road to Peace in Mozambique (1982-1992)*, CIIR Briefing Paper. London.

Wallace, T. (1990) 'Refugee Women: Their Perspectives and Our Responses', paper for the Institute of Social Studies, the Hague.

Weiss, T.G., and Minear, L. (1993) *Humanitarianism Across Borders: Sustaining Civilians in Times of War*. London: Lyne Rienner Publishers.

Welbourn, A. (1993) PRA, 'Gender and Conflict Resolution: Some Problems and Possibilities'. Paper for PRA and Gender Workshop, 6 and 7 December 1993, IDS Sussex.

Yusuf, A. (1993) *Somalia: The Roots of Reconciliation*, London: ACTIONAID.

Zartman (1985) *Ripe for Resolution* Oxford University Press, New York.

Zwi, A. and Ugalde A. (1989) 'Towards an Epidemiology of Political Violence in the Third World', *Social Science and Medicine*, Vol 28, No 7, pp 633-642, Pergamon.

Information on the organisations involved in the workshop

ACORD: A Consortium for Africa. ACORD (Agency for Co-operation and Research in Development) is a broad-based, international consortium of non-governmental organisations. The Consortium is independent of political and religious affiliations, and works under the trusteeship of its member agencies, in partnership with its field teams and local communities in Africa.

ACORD's main role is to help to establish or strengthen local, non-governmental structures with a view to promoting self-reliant participatory development. At the same time, ACORD also acts in emergency situations which seem likely to give rise to new development needs. Given the turbulence in Africa, ACORD finds itself working more and more in assisting local communities to survive through emergencies and rehabilitation to the time when longer-term development can take place.

ACORD, Francis House, Francis Street, London SW1P 1DQ. Tel: 0171 828 7611/7612; Fax: 0171 976 6113; Telex: 8954437 ACORD G; E-mail: acord@gn.org.apc

The School of Public Policy, University of Birmingham: The School's role is to act as a bridge between the worlds of practice and of academic research and education. The School provides postgraduate and undergraduate education, management development courses, short practical training programmes, research, and consultancy services across several spheres of public and voluntary service management policy. Two of the four departments in the school are The Centre for Urban and Regional Studies (CURS), which specialises in issues of urban and regional policy, particularly housing, local economic development, tourism, leisure and welfare services; and The Development Administration Group (DAG), which seeks to promote effective management and good governance in developing and transitional countries, giving special attention to urban, rural, and financial management.

School of Public Policy, University of Birmingham, Edgbaston, Birmingham B15 2TT. Tel: 0121 414 5021 (CURS) and 0121 414 4987 (DAG). Fax: 0121 414 3279 (CURS) and 0121 414 4989 (DAG).

Responding to Conflict: Responding to Conflict is a not-for-profit training and consultancy unit based in the Selly Oak Colleges Federation, Birmingham. It was set up in September 1991 to enable organisations working for development, human rights, and peace in situations of instability and conflict to function more effectively, whether in providing essential services or in promoting just and sustainable change. Through various activities, including an 11-week intensive and practical international course entitled Working with Conflict, Responding to Conflict facilitates the sharing of conflict-handling skills and experience across cultures and continents, and seeks to stimulate innovative thinking and action, particularly at community level.

Responding to Conflict, 1046 Bristol Road, Birmingham B29 6LJ. Tel: 0121 415 5641. Fax: 0121 415 4119.

www.ingramcontent.com/pod-product-compliance
Ingram Content Group UK Ltd.
Pitfield, Milton Keynes, MK11 3LW, UK
UKHW051825020626
6192IPUK00005B/55